PRAIS

WHO KILLED THE C/

"Jack Granatstein has eloque
preparedness and role in the world anu ὓ.
that any literate Canadian could easily digest, in the interests of keeping Canada strong and free."

—*Canadian Military History*

"A stunning monograph, short without being sketchy. Exactly
what you'd want from a scholar who's engaged."

—John Robson, *The Ottawa Citizen*

"There is nothing wrong with a knowledgeable and well-
argued polemic: a history with a point is a big improvement
on history without a point. . . . Students will eat it up."

—Mark Proudman, H-Canada

"A convincing analysis of Canada's embrace of a delusional
foreign policy that equates knee-jerk anti-Americanism
with sovereignty."   —*Books in Canada*

"Aimed directly at the general public, but will no doubt have
scores of professionals scribbling furiously in denial or
support."   —*Policy Options*

"A wake-up call for both elected officials and ordinary citizens. . . . It may very well be now or never for the future of
our nation's military preparedness."

—*Veritas* (Royal Military College Club)

J. L. GRANATSTEIN is the author of over sixty books, including *Who Killed Canadian History?*, *Yankee Go Home?*, and *Victory 1945* (with Desmond Morton). *The Generals* won the J. W. Dafoe Prize and the UBC Medal for Canadian Biography. The Royal Society of Canada awarded him the J. B. Tyrrell Historical Gold Medal (1992) for "outstanding work in the history of Canada." In 1996, the Conference of Defence Associations Institute named him winner of the Vimy Award. In 1997, he received the Order of Canada. A Distinguished Research Professor of History Emeritus at York University, he has received honorary degrees from the University of Western Ontario and the University of Calgary, and from Memorial, McMaster, and Ryerson universities. He is a member of the RMC Board of Governors and Chair of the Council for Canadian Security in the 21st Century.

Who Killed
the Canadian Military?

Who Killed
the Canadian Military?

J.L. GRANATSTEIN

Harper*Perennial*Canada   A PHYLLIS BRUCE BOOK

For MJHG
Who would not have agreed

Published by Phyllis Bruce Books,
an imprint of HarperCollins Publishers Ltd

First published in hardcover by Phyllis Bruce Books and Harper*Flamingo*Canada,
imprints of HarperCollins Publishers Ltd, 2004.
First paperback edition: 2004.
This paperback edition: 2008.

Third Edition

HarperCollins books may be purchased for educational, business,
or sales promotional use through our Special Markets Department.

HarperCollins Publishers Ltd
2 Bloor Street East, 20th Floor
Toronto, Ontario, Canada
M4W 1A8

www.harpercollins.ca

ISBN 978-1-55468-301-7

Library and Archives Canada Cataloguing in Publication is available.

TC 9 8 7 6 5 4 3 2 1
Printed and bound in Canada

Contents

Introduction
to the Third Edition

MUCH HAS CHANGED in Canadian defence policy since this book first appeared in 2004. First, there has been a new government in power in Ottawa since February 2006, and Prime Minister Stephen Harper's Conservative Party has invested substantially more money in defence than its predecessors. The highlights among a myriad of procurement decisions have been the acquisition of four heavy lift C-17 aircraft and orders for new Hercules aircraft, the purchase of new (if slightly used) Leopard C-2 tanks from the Dutch, new M-777 artillery, orders for new medium trucks, and the decision to acquire naval vessels that can navigate the ice in the low Arctic, the latter a large part of a promised but still undefined "Canada First" strategy. The 2007–08 defence budget, including supplementary estimates, came in at $18.4 billion or 1.3 percent of the Gross Domestic

Product. This represented a substantial increase, a major improvement, in a short period of time, and it was an indication that the Tories took their campaign promises seriously.

The new government has been less successful, however, in increasing the size of the Canadian Forces by a promised ten thousand regulars. The problem is not with recruitment—which is apparently going well—but with the retirement from the Canadian Forces of officers and men and women who are opting to take their pensions. The problem is also compounded by the lack of training instructors, most especially in the army, to bring the new recruits up to standard.

The reason for the training system's weaknesses is Canada's active participation in the Afghan War, the driving force in defence policy since 2005. The battlefield demands of the war, along with the rotation of 2,500 troops every six months, puts severe strains on the manpower of the regular and reserve forces, and many instructors have had to be pulled off the job for deployment abroad.

The key domestic event that stepped up the Canadian role in the war came about in 2005, when the Liberal government of Paul Martin selected Rick Hillier to be Chief of the Defence Staff. Dynamic, charismatic, and determined to make the Canadian Forces combat-capable once more, General Hillier somehow persuaded Defence Minister Bill Graham, never known for his hawkishness, to get more funding for the CF and to accept a combat deployment in

Kandahar. Graham and Hillier then persuaded the prime minister, another whose commitment to the military virtues had hitherto gone unnoticed, to agree. Instead of doing quasi-peacekeeping duty in Kabul, the Afghan capital, the army would move to Kandahar in February 2006 for a one-year mission that aimed to fight the Taliban in the south of Afghanistan and, with a Provincial Reconstruction Team, work on development. The commitment involved the troops on the ground and a substantial deployment of air (and sometimes sea) resources to support the mission.

In May 2006, soon after it came to power, the Harper government went to Parliament and narrowly won approval to extend the mission by two years to February 2009. As I write this, Harper is seeking to extend the mission to the end of 2011 if conditions, as laid out in the report of an Independent Panel led by former Liberal deputy prime minister John Manley, are met.

The Afghan mission has been costly—78 soldiers killed in action or in accidents and some 300 wounded to February 2008, and it has not been very popular with the Canadian public, especially francophones. There were widespread media predictions that when the Royal 22e Régiment went to Kandahar in the summer of 2007 for its six-month deployment and suffered casualties, there would be a firestorm against the federal government in Quebec. The Vandoos and sub-units in its Battle Group did suffer casualties, but the public's unhappiness seemed to be mixed almost equally with pride in the performance of French Canada's soldiers. And when the dead landed at Canadian Forces Base Trenton in Ontario and were convoyed to Toronto for autopsies, Ontarians solemnly lined the overpasses on Highway 401 to honour them just as they had done for anglophone casualties. The war in Afghanistan, the war for the hearts and minds of Canadians, goes on.

I admit that I have difficulty accepting the rationales offered by those Canadians who oppose the mission in Kandahar. That they hate to see Canadians dying is understandable; we all do. That they believe we are in Afghanistan only to let Prime Minister Stephen Harper serve President George W. Bush's foreign policy is, while incorrect, understandable. An independent nation needs a foreign policy that serves its national interests, and if our leaders do not bother to talk to the citizens about what those interests are, no one should be surprised if Canadians reach for the simplest explanation for every problem and every government decision.

Many Canadians, not least those who support the New Democratic Party, have come to call Afghanistan "Stephen Harper's war." Well, Harper is the prime minister, and he must prosecute the war that he supports. But for purely partisan reasons, the NDP and too many other Canadians, including what on most days seems to be a left-leaning majority of the Liberal caucus, have forgotten that the Martin government put us into Kandahar knowing full well that the mission entailed combat and casualties.

I can at least comprehend these positions. Where I have a real problem is with those critics of the war who refuse to accept that Canadian troops in Kandahar are there as part of a North Atlantic Treaty Organization–led force operating under a United Nations mandate. This puzzles me, and so does the failure to recognize that the Afghan government and, according to opinion polls, the Afghan people want us there. There are whole faculties of legal scholars trying to demonstrate that the UN resolution authorizing the mission has been misinterpreted or is illegal. Fortunately, statements at the end of January 2008 by UN Secretary-General Ban Ki-moon will put a crimp in these arguments—or should. These same pro-UN supporters rejoiced in 2003 when Canada stayed out of Iraq because the Security Council did not consent to the war. But now that the UN has spoken on Afghanistan, the critics still shout anti-Bush and anti-Harper slogans.

Can calling our soldiers "baby-killers" be far behind? It is only a matter of time, I fear. The anti-war movement—I use that term deliberately to emphasize the link to the Vietnam War forty years ago—has begun to move onto university campuses to block job fair representation by the Canadian

Forces. At the University of Victoria on January 30th this year, some twenty students and a group of "Raging Grannies," a seniors' movement particularly virulent on the West Coast, armed with a cardboard tank and a flag-draped coffin, blocked access to the CF display. The service personnel reacted calmly (despite having paid for their table with your tax dollars), but some students believed that the protest interfered with their right to free speech and their right to see what the CF had to offer. Of course these students were correct, but we can expect this kind of protest to spread. The University of Western Ontario is already trying to restrict "military-related" research.

The simple truth is that Afghanistan is not analogous to Vietnam. Nor is it the same as the Iraq War. The Americans and South Vietnamese people lost in Vietnam. The Americans won on the battlefield in Iraq in 2003, but their lack of planning for what came after military victory and the factionalism and religious strife in Iraq that resulted have pushed that conflict close to the tipping point five years later. Both of those struggles produced and will produce major political and military changes in the United States. Lost battles can do that.

But the Afghan War is not lost. Militarily, the Taliban cannot stand and fight (as it tried to do against the Canadians' Task Force Orion in the summer of 2006). Yes, the insurgents can use improvised explosive devices (IEDs) and suicide bombers, but those are pinpricks, however costly in lives, that smack almost of military desperation. No, the Hamid Karzai government is not as democratic as Canadians and their allies would like. Yes, the opium poppies flourish, and warlords and corrupt officials skim off their full share. Yes, the Pakistan border is porous, leaking fresh Taliban daily into Afghanistan. Yes, prisoners are tortured by their Afghan jailers. It's all true, but for a medieval state struggling to enter the modern world, such things, although regrettable, are to be expected.

Not condoned, not accepted, but expected. Canadians must remember that President Karzai heads a sovereign state, however weak its grasp, and there are limits to what the allied forces and governments can do. We can push and prod Kabul toward democratic reforms—and we should— but the Afghans themselves must decide to change their ways. For example, those Canadians who object to Afghan troops, operating with Canadians in the field, taking Taliban prisoners are simply missing the point. Mentored by Canadian officers and warrants they may be, but the Afghan soldiers respond to their own chain of command and government, and rightly so. If Taliban prisoners are tortured, that is the Afghan government's responsibility—until such time as our Western practises can be inculcated into the Afghan justice system. Similarly, those Canadians who now argue that the Charter of Rights and Freedoms should instantly and automatically apply to every Taliban prisoner touched by a Canadian soldier are deliberately playing foolish games with Canadian lives.

Indeed, the whole detainee issue in Canada is a deadly con game. Every complaint of torture, spurious or not, is treated as credible. The governor of Kandahar personally tortured me, one prisoner says, and the Canadian media goes wild. Whether the charge is credible matters not a whit. The aim of those in Canada spreading the charges is clear: discredit the Afghan government, discredit the NATO-led force, discredit the Canadian troops and, if this cannot be done, then hamstring soldiers in the field with regulations and rules that hamper their ability to operate effectively. The same Canadians who preferred Saddam to Bush now sometimes appear to favour the Taliban over the Canadian and NATO forces.

Lenin supposedly called those Western capitalists who supported his Communist regime in Russia "useful idiots." We have similar folk with us today. Jack Layton says that we cannot win in Afghanistan. No invading army, he says, has ever won there, and we should get out now and let the United Nations send in peacekeepers—an unhistorical position that, even if delivered with his usual wide-eyed innocent look, is flatly wrong and wholly disgraceful. Good thing the democracies didn't listen to his ilk after Dunkirk. What the NDP stand, if implemented, would do to Canadian credibil-

ity in Washington, in NATO, and in the United Nations—
what it would do to the Afghan people who would be abandoned to the mercy of the Taliban—seems beyond Layton's
understanding.

For months Stéphane Dion and his Liberal caucus called
for Canadians to conduct development and possibly military
training of the Afghan National Army, but not to engage in
combat under any circumstances, except perhaps self-
defence—wherever that position might leave them. Just how
those useful roles can be carried on in the combat zone that is
Kandahar without Canadian deaths, how development can
proceed without security in place, is left unstated. There is no
elaboration of the Grit position because there can be none
that makes sense. Deputy leader Michael Ignatieff tries to
talk sensibly about the war, but few in the Liberal caucus
appear willing to listen. Certainly Dion does not want to
hear what his past rival for the leadership has to say.

Academics get into the game too. Let me cite one only. The
holder of a prestigious Canada Research Chair, Michael
Byers of the Liu Centre at the University of British Columbia,
makes no bones about his pro-NDP position, and he is
omnipresent in the media, regularly denouncing the Afghan
struggle as "Stephen Harper's war." To Byers, Canada
should be out of "a failing counter-insurgency mission" in
Afghanistan. "It's time to move NATO troops out, and UN
peacekeepers in," he said. And "then, let's get serious about

the 'responsibility to protect' where it's needed most"—in Darfur, a part of Sudan.

That Darfur is a tragedy is clear. That Canadians could do anything to ameliorate the slaughter that has been aided and abetted by the government in Khartoum is far less evident. Byers—who plainly knows nothing about the military—forgets that Darfur's desert conditions and lack of infrastructure make a massive logistical effort a pre-condition for any Canadian commitment. Shortages of aircraft, equipment, and personnel make it unlikely for the Canadian Forces to be able to carry off a mission successfully (in contrast to Kandahar, where we have been able to piggyback on the massive U.S. military infrastructure at the huge airfield there). Nor is Darfur the simple "blue beret" peacekeeping that Byers appears to assume. There would be Canadian casualties in Sudan, perhaps as many as we have suffered in Kandahar, and any troops deployed there will require heavy weaponry. Then there is the opposition of the Sudanese government to permitting many Western troops on their (bitterly contested) terrain.

But the "Darfur good, Kandahar bad" mantra goes on without cessation. Somehow, saving the women and children of Darfur has become more important to Byers and the NDP than saving the women and children of Afghanistan. I am not sure why this is, why one Sudanese woman is more valuable than one Afghani child, except that the United States is committed on the ground in Afghanistan and everything American is evil to some Canadians. If I could, I'd like to save both the Darfuri and the Afghans—but Afghanistan has invited us in and Khartoum appears very reluctant to let us enter. Realistically, the choice has been made for us.

Realism is the key to all this. We need to recognize that Canada is a small nation with very small numbers of military personnel. There are realistic limits to what we can do on our own or even in alliance with our friends. We have a nation that is perpetually divided along French-English lines on military questions. We have an anti-American streak in our character that sometimes serves us poorly and makes us forget our own national interests. And we have an over-developed moralism that makes us preachy in the extreme, certain of our rectitude, at least when compared to that of our southern neighbour.

But we are in Afghanistan to serve our own national interests in shutting down a terrorist haven and rebuilding a failed state. If we can help bring a better governmental system, aid and education, and perhaps even a variant of freedom to a part of the world that has not known these things before, well and good. Realism demands nothing less than that we try.

xix

JLG
Toronto, February 2008

Introduction

"**W**HAT do you do, soldier?" the traditional question
goes. "I kill people and blow things up," the soldier
replies. Such brutal honesty would shock most Canadians.
"But you're peacekeepers," Canadians would say with the
utmost dismay in their voices. "You keep peace and ease
troubled situations; you don't kill people." In the eyes of
their fellow citizens, the men and women of the Canadian
Forces are more like social workers than people who do the
hard, dirty work involved in protecting our national interests. The disconnect between the military and the politicians,
between the Canadian Forces and Canadians, is at the root
of the problem of our military today.

The globe is as dangerous as ever, with bloodshed in
Liberia and the Congo, Palestine and Israel, Iraq, Afghanistan, Indonesia, Sri Lanka, and fifty more hot spots. North

America itself is under threat from weapons of mass destruction, and Canada, despite the beliefs of its government leaders and large numbers of its citizens, is subject to attack by terrorists. Somehow, even after the horror of September 11, 2001, next door, Canadians continue to think that they live on an island of safety, that they are beloved by the world for their goodwill, tolerance, and humanitarianism. They believe that the Canadian Forces, though perhaps a little run down at the end of 2003 with an effective strength of only 54,000 personnel and obsolete equipment, including forty-year-old helicopters and Hercules transports, is still a major player in the world. Wasn't the unification of the army, navy, and air force a path-breaking success? Hasn't Canada led the way in putting women in combat roles and establishing quotas for visible minorities? Surely the Canadian policy of military bilingualism is unique?

That whole scenario is a fool's paradise. Canada has reached a new level of irrelevancy in foreign and military affairs. The nation might still belong to the G-8, the United Nations, the North Atlantic Treaty Organization (NATO), the Commonwealth, la Francophonie, and many more world organizations, but Canada has ceased to matter internationally. Shaky defence and foreign policies, pandering to political correctness at home and elsewhere, and too little money thrown too late at domestic and global problems have left a proud global legacy in ruins. "Soft power," former Foreign

Minister Lloyd Axworthy's lamentable policy to press Canada's values on the world, constituted the best Canada could come up with in the late 1990s.

In the cut-throat realm of international relations, power still comes primarily from the barrel of a gun, not from the ranks of social workers that Canadians believe they send abroad. The weakness of the Canadian military has played a part in limiting its ability to operate on foreign fields as well as in destroying the country's reputation in global capitals. Does this weakness serve Canada's national interests? Do we even know what these interests are? Or is Canada such a do-gooder that its interests are irrelevant and the projection abroad of its values—multiculturalism, good governance, respect for human rights, and so on—all that matters? Our government seems to believe that values are the most important tools in our diplomatic and military kitbags. We preach and posture, and Ottawa somehow thinks the world cares.

It was not always this way. There was a time when Canadians boasted they were always there in the pinch. We fought in the Great War from the outset, raising almost 650,000 men from a population of just 8 million between 1914 and 1918. The Canadian Corps, four divisions strong, earned an unparalleled reputation on the Western Front, and actions such as Ypres, Vimy, Passchendaele, and the Hundred Days will always ring with the cries of brave men doing great deeds. Canada's pilots—Billy Barker, Raymond Collishaw, and Billy Bishop, to name but three—led the way in the dog-fights over the trenches and were major players in winning the air war. In the Second World War, Canada put 1.1 million men and women into uniform between 1939 and 1945, or 10 percent of its population. The dominion sent what became the world's third largest navy to sea and fought the Battle of the Atlantic; raised the fourth largest air force, which attacked the enemy homeland and flew on every continent; and created the First Canadian Army of five divisions and two additional armoured brigades, which battled in Sicily, Italy, and France and liberated the Low Countries. At the same time, Canada produced huge quantities of goods from its fields and factories for the war effort and gave billions of dollars to its allies. Yet, almost ninety years after Vimy and sixty years after D-Day, most Canadians know nothing of their nation's role in the world wars.

They might be expected to know more about the Cold War and the post–Cold War disorder, but there is little evidence that Canadians do. In the post-1945 period, Canada provided NATO with a first-rate infantry brigade group, an air division of fighter jets, and a well-equipped fleet that included aircraft carriers, submarines, and some of the world's most sophisticated surface warships. It fought and eventually helped to win the Cold War in Western Europe. With an army, navy, and air force numbering 120,000 regulars and a large-sized reserve at its post-war peak in the 1950s, the nation sent troops and ships to the Korean War between 1950 and 1953. It boasted ever after that Canada was always ready and willing when the United Nations called for peacekeepers. Lester Pearson won the Nobel Peace Prize for his efforts in creating the UN Emergency Force after the 1956 Suez Crisis, and many Canadians believed their role in the world had at last been properly recognized.

For years, they revelled in the idea that their nation was the only one that had served on every peacekeeping mission. Not any more. Canada today ranks thirty-fourth in the provision of troops for UN peacekeeping, well behind developing countries such as Bangladesh, Fiji, or Senegal. We've become no better in working with "coalitions of the willing" in small wars for limited aims. Claiming its "peace dividend" and beginning a long process of budget-cutting and reductions in strength before and after the end of the long confrontation with the Soviet Union, Canada pulled its land and air forces out of NATO in Europe. Although Ottawa scrambled to dispatch fighter aircraft and ships to the first Gulf War in 1990–91, it could not send an army brigade because we had no modern tanks or other heavy equipment able to keep pace with the American, British, and French coalition members. A few years later, Canada sent the Canadian Airborne Regiment to Somalia, a mission that ended in the murder of a local youth and a scandal that almost killed the Canadian Forces. The problems that beset the armed forces, a product of years of insufficient funding and weak political and military leadership, could no longer be ignored. But once the Somalia inquiry was done, the country turned away to focus on other issues. The Canadian Forces simply didn't matter to political leaders concerned with the budget deficit above all else.

Canada managed to send an infantry battalion to Afghanistan after the al-Qaeda attacks on September 11, 2001, began the War on Terrorism—but with the wrong uniforms and with air and ground transport begged and borrowed from the United States. When four soldiers tragically died in a "friendly fire" incident at the hands of US Air Force pilots, the country wallowed in anti-American sentiment. Perhaps that helped to explain why we chose not to participate, or even to support the United States, in the Iraq War of 2003. In the summer of that year we sent more troops to Afghanistan, and Ottawa claimed that was sufficient. As it turned out, the understaffed and overcommitted Canadian Forces could not even do the job the Chrétien government volunteered them for, and Canada had to ask NATO to take over the mission and provide specialist units for the operation in Kabul.

Now our role in North American homeland defence, like our position on the Iraq War, sometimes seems deliberately designed to provoke Washington rather than work with the United States to ease its legitimate post–September 11 security concerns. Anti-Americanism at every level of government, scepticism in the media, and Canadians' dislike of President George W. Bush are all very powerful in Canada. No one seems to care that these attitudes threaten our trade links with the most powerful economy on earth (not to mention the three in ten Canadian jobs and the more than 40 percent of gross domestic product dependent on Canada–US trade), as well as the military relationship on which we depend completely for our ultimate security.

Not surprisingly, other countries have noticed Canada's shaky policies and military failings. The Americans, most notably, are furious because geography, placing us atop the air routes to the United States and creating the long un-defended border between us, gave Canada a major role to play in the defence of North America. They have held off overt retaliation against the government on the assumption that the new Liberal prime minister in 2003, Paul Martin, might be better than the hapless Jean Chrétien. The British and even the French consider the Canadian Forces a joke, and British troops in the former Yugoslavia in the early 1990s called the Canadians, whose two battalions there were organized into units called Canbat 1 and Canbat 2, the "Can'tbats." Though no slur against the soldiers, who were very capable, the nickname was no compliment to our policy-makers in Ottawa or to the restrictions that crippled our servicemen in the field with rules and regulations. With only

7

a handful of Canadians attached to NATO today and with the navy, still the most up-to-date and effective Canadian service, tied up at quayside in Halifax and Victoria, our European allies scarcely acknowledge our military utility or our existence any more.

How did we reach this point of utter irrelevance? What choices, what sins of omission and commission, erased the well-earned Canadian military reputation that was won in hard fighting at Paardeberg, Vimy, the Canal du Nord, Ortona, the Scheldt, and Kap'yong? Who is responsible? How much of the blame are you, the citizens of Canada, prepared to accept?

In *Who Killed the Canadian Military?* my focus will be on the politicians who did the damage. Yes, some generals were venal, more interested in their perks than in caring for their troops; yes, some officers made unprincipled decisions that, in hindsight, were foolish. But in the end, most of the military miscreants have had their careers terminated or blighted. The politicians, in contrast, slashed budgets with a will but avoided taking any responsibility for their terrible decisions. Our elected leaders failed to secure the necessary budgets and equipment for the Canadian Forces, even as they dispatched the nation's heavily stressed servicemen and women into dangerous situations around the world to serve their political ends. Many, even most, of these politicians have gone on to greater rewards and the acclaim of their compatriots; certainly none has suffered. Blame should be directed not only at self-serving generals and bureaucrats but at the elected representatives too. Blame also ought to be fixed on you, the voters, who unquestioningly elected and re-elected these politicians without challenging their decisions.

How can we remake Canadian military policy and restore the Canadian Forces so they can once again play a role that serves the nation, defends our country against terrorism, and makes our people proud? Who killed the Canadian military? How can we give the Canadian Forces life again? This book will answer these questions.

Let me sound a personal note in the belief that readers have the right to know the direction from which I come. I served in the Canadian Army as a cadet at Le Collège militaire royal de St-Jean and at the Royal Military College of Canada and as a very junior officer for the ten years from 1956 to 1966. Happily no one ever fired a shot at me, I was never near danger, and most of my service was safely behind a desk. My experiences occasionally will appear on these pages.

More relevant than my own inglorious military service is that I have studied Canada's military history for many years and written extensively about it. I have taken part in the public debates on Canadian military policy for more than thirty years, and today I am the chair of the Council for Canadian

Security in the 21st Century, a pro-defence lobby group. If the choice is, as the old economist's saying goes, for guns or butter, then I guess I'm for guns. In a country as rich as ours, I believe we can have both. Without the guns, someone just might come along to take our butter away.

One final note: this book went to press in December 2003. Events that occurred after this date are addressed in the new introduction that precedes this one, and in the afterword at the end of this book.

CHAPTER 1

Fatal Distraction: Lester Pearson and the Unwarranted Primacy of Peacekeeping

Who killed the Canadian military? Lester B. Pearson—inadvertently. Canadians have been enamoured with the idea of peacekeeping ever since Secretary of State for External Affairs Pearson won the Nobel Prize in 1957 for his role in establishing the United Nations Emergency Force (UNEF), the UN's first large peacekeeping force, in November 1956. Created during the Suez Crisis, UNEF separated the invading armies of the British, French, and Israelis from the Egyptians and tried to freeze a situation in a troubled region while diplomats sought a lasting resolution.

What could possibly be wrong with peacekeeping? Canadians clearly like the concept; our soldiers, sailors, and airmen and women do it extremely well; and the government obviously views it as the employment of choice for the Canadian Forces. But . . .

It's the "but" that begins to raise problems. What no one remembers any longer is that, when "Mike" Pearson cobbled the force together, few in Canada cheered. Pearson's efforts at the United Nations in New York won scant praise from those who denounced him for selling out Canada's two mother countries. The British and the French believed they were resisting "a new Hitler" in Egypt's Colonel Gamal Abdel Nasser. At home, the Liberal minister faced denunciations from some Progressive Conservatives for siding with the United States against Britain, and Prime Minister Louis St. Laurent's statement that the days of "the supermen" of Europe were over only fuelled the controversy. Some analysts even suggested that Pearson's role in New York helped John Diefenbaker's Tories defeat the Liberals in the 1957 election. But when Pearson was awarded the Nobel Prize, the mood changed almost at once. Peacekeeping was now Canada's very own contribution to the world.

Yet Pearson's prize had a harmful effect on the Canadian military because it began the process whereby Canadians viewed their soldiers as the world's natural peacekeepers, well trained, well equipped, instinctively impartial, and fair. There was some truth in that description in the 1950s and 1960s, when the Canadian military *was* well trained and well equipped and Canadians went off to Lebanon, the Congo, West New Guinea, Yemen, the Arab-Israeli borderlands, and Cyprus. They served well in trying to prevent small conflicts from exploding into large wars. But Canadians never really understood what their peacekeepers were doing, why they were good at their jobs, and why they were needed. And because they fell in love with peace-keeping, Canadians began to fall out of love with the true purpose of a military—to be ready to fight wars.

Canada had been part of NATO since April 1, 1949, a charter member of the Western alliance united against Soviet expansionism. Prime Minister St. Laurent had campaigned in Quebec to muster support for the alliance and helped to create a huge majority in the House of Commons for adhesion to the North Atlantic Treaty. From 1950 on, he had also supported the nation's rearmament. Canada had fought two world wars overseas in the first half of the twentieth century, and Canadians understood that collective security and defence mattered. The horrors of the past strongly shaped their present.

The country's armed forces in the mid-1950s, when St. Laurent and Pearson worked closely together, reflected this belief that the military was important and necessary. The army, some 50,000 strong, was a balanced force with infantry, armour, and artillery, but also with the skills in logistics, engineering, and communications required for complex operations abroad. Canada had a fleet, including an aircraft carrier that, in a pinch, could be used to carry the army's heavy equipment, and it had squadrons of transport aircraft, the aircrews to fly them, and the ground crews to

15

maintain them. In 1955 the three Canadian armed services, all well equipped and well trained, numbered 118,000 and, two years before, cost an incredible 7.8 percent of the gross domestic product of just over $20 billion (compared to a pathetic 1.1 percent in 2003). Few other medium-sized countries acceptable to the UN's member states and secretariat had those capabilities. Canadians, moreover, could operate in French as well as in English. That made our peacekeepers very useful in the Cold War when the Great Powers—the United States and the Soviet Union—and major powers with colonialist pasts such as Britain and France, all with large military forces, were not acceptable in UN operations to the majority of members.

Not that Canada, the old Canada, was always acceptable to everyone. The Egyptians in 1956 had balked at Canadian participation in the UN Emergency Force, even if Pearson had saved Cairo's destruction by proposing it. The Canadians were part of NATO, along with the British and French invaders. Their flag, the now all-but-forgotten Red Ensign, had a Union Jack in the corner. Their soldiers wore British-pattern battle-dress uniforms. Worse still, the infantry battalion initially chosen for UNEF service was the British-sounding Queen's Own Rifles, not the fictitious East Kootenay Anti-Imperialist Brigade that Pearson wryly conceded later would have been more appropriate. The other available units had equally imperial names—the Princess

Patricia's Canadian Light Infantry (PPCLI), the Royal Canadian Regiment, the Black Watch (Royal Highland Regiment of Canada), and the Royal 22e Régiment.

It took extraordinary efforts to get President Nasser to agree to Canadian participation in UNEF, and Pearson told the Egyptian Ambassador to the UN: "We had even been careful to exclude from the force any Canadians with noticeably English accents." For all that extraordinary Canadian self-abnegation, the Queen's Own Rifles, their lineage, uniforms, and flag an affront to Cairo, never made it to UNEF, as an armoured reconnaissance squadron and less-malevolently titled (but perhaps even more useful) logistical units took their place.

The Canadian contingent and its vehicles arrived at Port Said aboard the carrier HMCS *Magnificent*, proudly flying the same White Ensign as Britain's Royal Navy. The Egyptians, reasonably enough, threatened to sink the ship, which was itself scarcely distinguishable from a vessel of the Royal Navy, and the American officer in charge of clearing the Suez Canal had to contact *Magnificent*'s captain and beg him to haul down his colours. At the last possible minute, matters were smoothed over, but the whole episode was humiliating to the Royal Canadian Navy, Canada, and Pearson. The Secretary of State for External Affairs did not forget and, when he became Prime Minister seven years later, he set out to get Canada a distinctive Canadian flag and, more

17

hesitantly, to support the integration and unification of the three Canadian forces as a way to minimize their too-obvious British connections.

Several factors made Canada eager to participate in the Middle East and in other peacekeeping operations. As a Western power and a member of NATO, Canada had a vital national interest in holding off the Soviet threat. During the Suez Crisis, the split between Britain and France—the aggressors—and the United States was huge. Canada's actions were directed as much to repairing the breach among allies as to restoring peace in the area. Indeed, the two goals were positively inseparable. Anything else played into Moscow's meddling hands. In the former Belgian Congo in 1960, to cite another example, East and West were beginning to battle for a resource-rich area, one key explanation for the Canadian peacekeeping commitment there. In Cyprus in 1964, where Britain had bases and interests in a former colony, two NATO members, Greece and Turkey, were on the verge of war over the island they both wanted to control. Prime Minister Pearson was initially dubious about sending Canadian troops—"Let them cut each other up," he told Paul Hellyer, his Defence Minister. "We certainly won't go in just to help the British." A war would have had disastrous effects on NATO's southern flank, however, and External Affairs Minister Paul Martin Sr. went to work on the telephone, calling foreign ministers around the world. In his memoirs, he wrote: "The result of my phone calls was the establishment of the UN force . . . I telephoned a rather surprised [UN Secretary General] U Thant to tell him the good news." The Prime Minister too must have been surprised at Martin's success, and Martin likely exaggerated his own role, but Pearson did secure Parliament's approval on March 13, 1964. Canada sent an infantry battalion at once, and UNFICYP, the United Nations Force in Cyprus, hit the ground running. This solution served Canada's desire to be a peacekeeper, but it also saved a critical part of the Western alliance, exactly as in 1956.

President Lyndon Johnson, worried about NATO's future if the Greeks and the Turks went to war, was grateful. As Pearson recalled in his memoirs, LBJ "was amazed and filled with admiration . . . and I think this may have changed his attitude toward Canada . . . 'You'll never know what this may have prevented.'" The President then asked, "Now what can I do for you?" Although Pearson replied "nothing at the moment," I believe that Johnson's willingness to agree to the Auto Pact the next year, an agreement that hugely benefited Canada's auto sector, may well have been Pearson's reward for Cyprus.

For most of the Cold War, peacekeeping brought public huzzahs for the Canadian Forces but few military benefits. The generals, air marshals, and admirals saw UN service as a distraction from their main task of preparing to defeat Soviet tank armies on the central German plain, defending North America from nuclear-armed long-range Russian bombers, and fighting Soviet submarines in the North Atlantic. Though peacekeeping never employed more than a few thousand men and was not a high military priority, it used up scarce military resources of bilingual army signallers or pilots of small aircraft, for example, and interfered with the training of the army, navy, and air force for war—or so the generals said. Moreover, to many senior officers, peacekeeping fostered a naïve attitude among both their men and the Canadian public alike: that, by simply donning a blue beret, Canadian soldiers could bring peace where only war or civil war had prevailed.

Canadians on peacekeeping missions reacted in their own different ways to their duties. Some in the 1950s and 1960s resented being shunted off to what they considered sideshows. There was no guarantee of promotion for working on UN missions and not much good training for real soldiering either. A young officer serving with the Royal Canadian Dragoons in the United Nations Emergency Force in 1962 wrote in a personal letter to me that he found the constant patrols in armoured cars in the Sinai very frustrating. "Funny thing about coming off the desert," he said sardonically, "everyone feels like a big party and has a tremendous itch to shoot up the local Bedouin police post."

Another Canadian, an Army Service Corps captain serving

in UNEF and based in Gaza and Port Said, wrote to me that "the Canadian appears to be the world's most provincial animal" when compared to Swedes, Danes, or Indians, with "closed minds, complete ignorance [and no] desire to learn or accept another's point of view . . ." Yet this same officer, after observing that "boredom is a place much like Port Said," added hopefully that, at UNEF's Gaza headquarters, "it's quite a sight on Sunday nights to see saris, turbans, business suits, fezes, etc. A very good feeling. The brotherhood of man is a possibility." In 1967, however, Egypt and Israel went to war again, and the Egyptians expelled the Canadian peacekeeping troops just before fighting began. The brotherhood of man? Or a political failure to seize the opportunity provided by a peacekeeping freeze to settle a crisis?

The hard realities of crisis resolution never penetrated the mind of the Canadian public, yet the idealism of selfless service in the cause of peace made Canadians proud of their lead role in peacekeeping. Their politicians also enjoyed the accolades received at the UN Headquarters in New York, the clout and prestige Canada thought it won with the international bureaucracy and in foreign offices in return for its soldiers.* Liberal

21

---

*A Department of National Defence study in 1992, cited by US scholar Joseph Jockel, found that foreign interviewees and a few Canadians "indicated that peacekeeping was not a strong factor in national influence." But "most Canadians disagreed, saying it was of importance."

and Tory governments alike rushed to volunteer the Canadian military for every peacekeeping operation, and for a time Canada and Canadians proudly boasted that their nation had been a participant in every UN mission—and even in non-UN missions, especially the International Control Commissions in the former French Indochina after 1954. Foreign ministers began to hope that, if they called in their markers in the world capitals and at UN headquarters in New York, they too might create a peacekeeping force and help freeze a crisis. If they could then get the Prime Minister to agree to send Canadian troops, a Nobel Peace Prize might come their way too. After all, it had worked for Lester Pearson, hadn't it? Didn't the prize help him become Liberal leader and, later, Prime Minister?* Not even the casualties of UN service—116 Canadian servicemen have been killed on United Nations and other peacekeeping and peace enforcement duties since the first, Brigadier H.H. Angle, on the India-Pakistan border in 1950—put a damper on the idea.

In the decade after Pearson's Nobel Prize, as the Cold War continued and as the United States got itself embroiled in the morass of the Vietnam War, the Canadian public began to believe that peacekeeping was its métier. We were the world's

---

*Some believed that Lloyd Axworthy, Jean Chrétien's Foreign Minister in the late 1990s, actively sought a Nobel Prize for his work on the Landmines Treaty. Perhaps it wasn't only peacekeeping that set foreign ministers salivating.

master peacekeepers, the indispensable United Nations' players. The Americans, always bumptious and too aggressive, fought wars, but Canadians, nature's neutral middlemen, kept the peace. This idea became a mantra, a powerful one that successive governments never challenged. War was foreign to Canadian thinking, but peacekeeping was the natural role for us to play. With the attentive public, peacekeeping was do-goodism writ large. It was also a military role that differentiated us from the Americans, a huge boost for Canadian nationalism. And if some worried that Canadians weren't pulling their military weight in the Cold War, there was one easy answer: the nation's peacekeeping did not require huge armies, large fleets, and vast air forces. Only blue berets and a few blue helmets were needed to do good and make a contribution.

In truth, the Cold War meant that the Americans and the Russians could exercise a form of control over their friends and client states. Neither wanted ethnic groups to begin to slaughter each other and provoke intervention. "Behave yourself and do what Moscow or Washington tell you," or so the message seemed to be. Peacekeeping missions were relatively few, and most required only a small number of troops.

Canadians loved the idea, though President Nasser's expulsion of our troops from Egypt in 1967 put a damper on public enthusiasm for some time. So did the Trudeau government's rejection of a "helpful fixer" role for Canada at the beginning of the 1970s. Still, UN demands for peacekeepers continued to be made on Ottawa, as few other nations had the combination of military skills and resources that Canada did. By tacit agreement, neither the Russians nor the Americans sent their soldiers on UN missions. The British and the French had colonial pasts that often made them unwelcome in Africa and Asia, where most UN missions were needed. Canada became the indispensable nation—or so we thought.

What changed peacekeeping was the end of the Cold War in a few short years from 1989 to 1991. The collapse of the Soviet Union lifted Moscow's dead hand from Eastern Europe, unleashing nationalisms galore. The African and Asian states that had been areas of contention between East and West now felt free to pursue their own agendas. Instead of peace, a new world disorder erupted as ethnic tribes—Serbs and Croats, Hutu and Tutsi, and dozens more—sought their revenge for historical slights. Peacekeeping initially seemed to boom, with the United Nations dispatching tens of thousands of troops and a score of forces around the globe in the early 1990s. But a UN shoulder flash and a white-painted Jeep no longer seemed enough to maintain peace, as people fought to kill their tribe's ancient enemies. There was a genocidal war in the former Yugoslavia, and UN forces there, including Canadians, fought large-scale battles, often unavailing, to try to stop the massacres. The United Nations buckled under the strain, its organization and finances insufficient to handle the task, and informal coalitions and NATO began to pick up the hard challenges. Peacekeeping had turned into a combination of peace enforcement and peacemaking, and it soon became just another synonym for war.

What made the situation worse for everyone was the utter incompetence of the United Nations in running peacekeeping missions. The UN was an organization of nations with conflicting interests; it also had an inefficient bureaucracy (highly paid and tax-free though it was) both at its headquarters in New York and around the world. Simply put, the UN's Security Council, General Assembly, and myriad committees did not work. The United States thought it ought to run the organization, the Russians sulked, and the British and especially the French played their age-old games of cynical and self-interested diplomacy. The Arab states hated the Israelis. Developing countries schemed how best to squeeze conscience money from the rich states. The United Nations couldn't run an ice-cream stand, let alone operate peacekeeping and peace enforcement missions around the world.

Canadian military planners had to learn to work around UN's dysfunctional supply system and, for example, the organization's ceilings on equipment when the situation on the ground in Bosnia exposed Canadian troops to danger. The UN issued orders to bring only light weapons and to restrict the number of armoured vehicles, but Canadian generals sensibly decided that more robust means of self-defence were necessary. The Canadians came to the former Yugoslavia with more weapons in their kitbags than the United Nations had decreed. To cite another even more horrific example, the UN's "old boys' club" of incompetent officials, along with its inability to reinforce its tiny peacekeeping force in Rwanda, left the Canadian force commander, Major-General Roméo Dallaire, unable to prevent a monstrous genocide. Canadian Major-General Maurice Baril, the military adviser to both the UN's Secretary General and the UN's peacekeeping head, then Kofi Annan, tried his best to help his friend Dallaire, but to no avail. The United Nations had proven to be a weak reed, especially when it confronted the peace and security issues it was created to address. If the Security Council's veto-wielding members didn't care about an issue, nothing would happen. In Rwanda, the French and Americans didn't, and hundreds of thousands died as a result.

Canada was not alone in recognizing that other organizations had to take over key peace support and peace enforcement operations. When the UN failed abysmally in the former Yugoslavia, NATO stepped in; when Yugoslav President Slobodan Milosevic tried to crush the Kosovo Albanians, NATO fought and won a totally justifiable and necessary "humanitarian war" to stop a genocide in the making. In Afghanistan, after coalition military operations against al-Qaeda and the Taliban regime, an International

Security Assistance Force took the field, a de facto NATO operation, although one authorized by the United Nations. It was clear that peace enforcement, the toughest kind of peacekeeping permitted under Article VII of the UN Charter, worked best outside the UN, with a coalition of nations operating under a Security Council green light. UN peacekeeping soon became limited to the low end of the violence scale, to freezing a situation and to giving the parties to a conflict a breathing space. The United Nations couldn't— and shouldn't—do everything.

To be fair, some of the problems that beset UN peacekeeping were simply beyond easy resolution. The United Nations in 1994 ran eighteen peacekeeping operations with 80,000 soldiers from eighty-two countries. A few years before, the entire staff of the UN's Peacekeeping Operations Department consisted of six civilians and three military officers. Today, in mid-2003, with the UN running fifteen operations with just over 30,000 military personnel on duty (and almost 5,000 civilian police as well), matters are somewhat better, with 400 civilian and military personnel on the UN Peacekeeping staff and an Undersecretary General in charge of Peacekeeping Operations. A round-the-clock Situation Center has even replaced the answering machine that used to respond to field commanders calling from Bosnia and Croatia to New York for instructions after 5 p.m. Eastern Standard Time and on weekends.

The United Nations always pretended that all national armies were equal in their capabilities, so New York frequently took the troops that were on offer at any given moment, whether they were properly trained or equipped for the mission. What else could it do? Some national contingents proved absolutely incapable of operating well; others collapsed the moment they were fired on. Some devoted themselves to operating on the black market; others preyed on local civilians; and some, their troopers riddled with AIDS, spread disease everywhere they went. That the demoralized, dysfunctional, incompetent UN forces were able to perform at all in a few operations was a near-miracle.

Compounding matters, the United Nations pays countries US$1,000 per soldier per month to provide troops for peace support operations. This income likely explains why Bangladesh, for example, in May 2003 had 2,625 soldiers on UN duties; Senegal, 523; and Nigeria, 2,548. Unlike these countries, which use their troops to bolster their hard currency holdings, the Canadian Forces, which in May 2003 had 219 soldiers on UN duty, allowed its soldiers to keep the UN's monthly shilling. Because the military's pay was so low for so long, many soldiers eagerly sought UN service as a way of supplementing their income. In effect, Canadian soldiers were selling themselves for UN dollars.

Above all, there is the pernicious "feel good" effect of peacekeeping. For fifty-six years, ever since 1948, the United

Nations has had military observers in Kashmir. Despite the organization's best efforts, India and Pakistan have fought two wars over that disputed region and now, as both countries possess nuclear arms, they are as close to war as they have been in the last two decades. For thirty years Canadians served in Cyprus, patrolling the Green Line separating Greek and Turkish Cypriots, yet not until the Mulroney government announced it was pulling its troops out of the UN Force in Cyprus did the parties really begin to talk, though to no avail. Some Canadians served in Cyprus for six, seven, or eight 6-month tours of duty, and a few were reputed to have second families living in Nicosia. The Canadian Airborne Regiment fought a major battle against invading Turkish troops in 1974 and sustained—and inflicted—casualties in this fight with a NATO ally at the Nicosia airport.

Endless missions extended well beyond their original intended lifespan. In spite of pledges by politicians to seek a speedy solution, these delays are very damaging to the concept of peacekeeping. Everyone feels good when the peacekeepers go in, but no one benefits if they stay in place for a generation, with no prospect of resolution of the crisis that brought them there in the first place. Peacekeeping must not and cannot be an end in itself. Either it is accompanied by serious diplomatic efforts at a resolution or it should not be tried. If diplomacy fails, the peacekeepers should be withdrawn.

Despite all these difficulties, the Canadian people love

peacekeeping. When UN peacekeepers were awarded the 1988 Nobel Peace Prize, many Canadians truly believed the award was intended above all for their soldiers. Perhaps it is not surprising that the only national military monument erected in the nation's capital since the Second World War, its figures standing on a concrete island in front of the glass walls of the National Gallery of Canada, commemorates not those who fought in Korea or those hundreds of thousands who served in NATO and helped win the Cold War, but those Canadian servicemen and women who served in peacekeeping operations. "Reconciliation," the monument demands. Peacekeeping and peacekeepers deserve to be honoured, but it is even more striking what Canada's governments chose not to recognize.

Much like peacekeeping, the United Nations has been and continues to remain popular with Canadians. With their instinctive preference for multilateralist organizations that give Ottawa a place to shelter itself away from the relentless pressure of the bilateral Canada–US relationship, we rely on the UN in spite of all the evidence of its complete ineffectiveness to the contrary. The UN doesn't work, the critics say. Well, it should, Canadians respond. Unfortunately, it doesn't work, and there is no sign at all that the UN can be fixed. Canadians cannot pin their hopes for a better world on a flawed, crippled world body.

*　*　*

Canadians tend to blush, stammer, and scrape their feet in the dirt in embarrassment when they talk about subjects like democracy and freedom, but those ideals have been and remain very important. This nation has never gone to war for aggressive reasons—we are one of the few countries anywhere that can say that—but only to defend our own soil or to fight with our friends and stand up for concepts like democracy, freedom, and justice. It is our historic willingness to take up arms for just causes, far more than our interest in and support for peacekeeping (important as that concept is), that has helped to make Canada the country it is.

Pearson knew that fact well. He had served overseas in an army medical unit and as a pilot trainee in the Great War, worked as a diplomat in London and Washington in the Second World War, and been Canadian External Affairs Minister during the Korean War. He appreciated the role that the UN could play, but he was also one of the founders of NATO, and he was never a believer in peacekeeping above all other means of statecraft. Peacekeeping was a tool, a device to freeze a crisis while statesmen sought a political solution to resolve it. Pearson soon realized that the United Nations could not broker a peace in the Middle East, nor could it prevent future wars among Israel, Egypt, and the other Arab states. Suez in 1956 was a Canadian and Pearsonian triumph, something that could scarcely be replicated so long as the Cold War went on. Other peacekeeping operations followed it in the Congo, Cyprus, and other trouble spots, but the record of successful resolution of crises by the UN was slim to non-existent. Shrewd, clever, and a life-long student of international affairs, Pearson knew what he had achieved, realized it meant little, ultimately, unless it translated into a durable peace, and understood that the interposition of a UN force between belligerents was not the universal panacea.

Pearson also understood that it was important to have Parliament approve the commitment of forces to United Nations operations. He insisted on taking the Cyprus commitment to Members of Parliament and, though the troops were already in the air, he was willing to recall them if the House voted no. That punctiliousness has slipped away, and Parliament is no longer asked as a matter of course to approve overseas commitments. I think it should be, and it would be useful if the House of Commons Standing Committee on National Defence and Veterans Affairs, generally a knowledgeable committee, had to recommend in favour of a commitment before the question went to all MPs.

Pearson's 1956 triumph was misinterpreted by his fellow citizens, as they fell in love with the United Nations and peacekeeping and continue today to raise their blue-helmeted soldiers to the levels of icons and myth—Canada as the universally beloved, tolerant, and idealistic peacekeeping exemplar to the world. Being Canadians, however, they understand nothing of how dangerous and difficult peace-keeping and peacemaking have become in the last decade. Nor do they seem to realize that Canada in 2003 has just over two hundred soldiers on UN duties. Given their chronic lack of interest in the military, they do not know that the present Canadian Forces, with well under 55,000 trained soldiers, sailors, and airmen and women, are incapable of doing more for the UN because they are so thinly stretched and ill-equipped. Yet being Canadian, they accept the con-tradictory idea that the Canadian Forces remain the world's ideal peacekeepers, indispensable to the United Nations.

Canadians do not realize that the major reason the Canadian Forces have proven themselves capable of peace-keeping is that the nation trains its men and women for war. "There is no such thing as a Canadian 'peacekeeper,'" according to military historian Dr. Sean Maloney. "There are Canadian soldiers. Peacekeeping covers a small band in the spectrum of conflict. Canadian national security demands that we have an armed force capable of fighting." It is a tru-ism that a war-trained soldier can fight and also do peace-keeping. A peacekeeping-trained soldier, however, cannot fight in a war—at least, not without dying quickly. The coun-try's best-known soldier, Major-General Lewis MacKenzie, argues similarly against making the Canadian Forces into peacekeepers alone. "There will come a day when the govern-ment turns to the military and says: 'Okay, we need you to fight and kill people,'" but then, he warns, "the military will raise its hand and say: 'Sorry, we don't do that any more.'"

Pearson's success in resolving the Suez Crisis created the myth that Canada was the impartial, indispensable, and universally loved nation. It wasn't true in 1956 and it's not true now, but Canadians and their governments fell prey to this idea. The result was super-simplistic reasoning that failed to assess the realities of the world, substituting peacekeeping for rational thought. And peacekeeping came to have a devastating effect on the Canadian military. "Soft power," Foreign Minister Lloyd Axworthy called it, but a flaccid military was more like it.

Pearson did no wrong—indeed, he did his job as Canadian External Affairs Minister so well in 1956 that he deserved every one of the plaudits he received. There is a law of unintended consequences, nonetheless, and a compliant public and the eager politicians they elect have run the military into the ground, all the while prattling about peacekeeping as the most important role for the Canadian Forces. It wasn't Mike Pearson who helped kill the Canadian military; rather, the idea of peacekeeping that his Nobel Peace Prize made into Canada's national mission is the culprit.

CHAPTER 2

The Folly
of Anti-Americanism:
The Diefenbaker Interlude

WHO killed the Canadian military? John Diefenbaker. The Tory Prime Minister from 1957 to 1963 became the first Canadian leader since Robert Borden in 1911 to use anti-Americanism deliberately as a political and electoral tool. Worse, he focused his venom on the military arrangements and the weaponry that his country and the United States used to defend North America and Western Europe in the Cold War, then at its most dangerous. Diefenbaker poisoned the atmosphere between the two countries and set the pattern for subsequent leaders to follow.

Canada's military relationship with the United States scarcely existed until the Second World War loomed on the horizon. In 1938 President Franklin Delano Roosevelt came to Canada to receive an honorary degree from Queen's University in Kingston, Ontario. He used the occasion to say: "I give to you assurance that the people of the United States will not stand idly by if domination of Canadian soil is threatened. . . ." Prime Minister Mackenzie King had not known that Roosevelt would offer this unsolicited pledge, but a few days later, speaking in Woodbridge, Ontario, King gave his own reciprocal promise: "We, too, have our obligations as a good friendly neighbour, and one of them is to see that . . . our country is made as immune from attack or possible invasion as we can reasonably be expected to make it, and that . . . enemy forces should not be able to pursue their way, either by land, sea or air to the United States, across Canadian territory." Each nation recognized its obligations to the other's security, though Canada was much the greater beneficiary.

Those 1938 speeches reversed a long history of difficulties. The mythical "undefended border" of blessed memory and after-dinner speeches had scarcely existed for most of Canadian history. Canada lived in fear of a US invasion until the beginning of the twentieth century—and, among some at army headquarters in Ottawa, until the early 1930s. Canada was a British dominion, and its military followed British practices, not American ones. This model remained in place even after the Nazi armies defeated the British and the French and drove the British Expeditionary Force off the continent at Dunkirk in May and June 1940. With only 11 million people, Canada suddenly became Britain's ranking ally.

In the summer of 1940, Canada faced a real possibility of attack for the first time. If Britain fell, the Royal Navy could pass into Germany's hands; if that happened, an invasion would become a realistic threat. Submarine warfare and attacks by battleships of the Bismarck class on east coast ports threatened commerce in both Canada and the still-neutral United States. In the Pacific, Japan was bellicose and aggressive, a potential threat to the west coast of North America. The perilous military situation forced Canada and the United States closer together, and in August 1940 speeches no longer seemed sufficient as a basis for policy. Roosevelt invited King to meet him at Ogdensburg, New York, and the two men agreed in a few hours' discussion to create a Permanent Joint Board on Defence (PJBD), the first defensive arrangement between the two nations. In a stroke, Canada's security had been guaranteed if Britain should be obliged to capitulate. Canada had become an American military protectorate.

The ties established at Ogdensburg led to US forces being stationed in Canada, to a joint and sometimes difficult defence relationship in Newfoundland, to a joint Canada–US invasion of Kiska in the Aleutian Islands in 1943, and to the formation of the 1st Special Service Force, a joint elite unit. Had the invasion of Japan proceeded in late 1945, a Canadian division, organized and equipped to US standards, was slated to participate. At home, American generals tried to get the Canadians to agree to a unified command—in effect, complete operational control of Canadian forces engaged in the defence of their own country. Canadian resistance to this plan largely succeeded, but there was no doubt who the junior partner was in the new relationship. With the

39

peace, the PJBD continued in operation, and the wartime links were maintained.

Compared with Canada's military linkages to Britain during the war, the ties to the south were modest. Canadians fought in Italy as part of a British army and in Northwest Europe under Field Marshal Bernard Montgomery's Army Group. They used mainly British equipment, including British-pattern clothing and small arms, and Canadians persisted in wearing the heavy and uncomfortable British steel helmet even though the US model was lighter and gave more protection—and could even be adapted for cooking food over a fire! Canadians did employ the American-designed Sherman tank and the American-built landing ship tanks (LSTs), however, and were happy to receive air support from American-designed fighter aircraft.

Nonetheless, Canadians tended to sneer at American military prowess, training, and tactics in both the Second World War and Korea. Americans "bugged out" too readily, Canadian officers believed, and the US practices of attritional warfare and maintaining a continuous front over hill and dale were very different from the British-Canadian model of conserving lives and setting up all-round defences on the high ground. Defence Minister Brooke Claxton returned from a visit to the Korean front to say that "American expenditures of lives and ammunition are high according to our standards, higher than our people would be willing to accept." Still, the US ability to get supplies forward, not to mention the quality of American "chow," was much admired. In Korea, for example, the Canadians flatly refused "terrible" British and Australian rations and insisted on getting American food. "My soldiers," said Brigadier John Rockingham, the first Canadian commander there, had become used to US rations "and liked them very much."

Sheer American power impressed Canadian officers. The Royal Canadian Air Force might have fought under the Royal Air Force in the Second World War, but by 1950 it was already drawing closer to the US Air Force. Both air forces recognized that the air defence of North America against the possibility of a Soviet attack was a joint problem, and personal and professional ties among senior officers led to informal understandings between both countries' air defence commands. The Royal Canadian Navy (RCN) similarly recognized that its future lay more in cooperation with the US Navy than the Royal Navy. The superiority of American technology partly explained this shift, but primarily it came from recognition that the RCN responded to NATO's Supreme Allied Command Atlantic, based at Norfolk, Virginia, when it put to sea in search of submarines flying the Soviet Union's hammer and sickle. The sea and air defence of Canada depended on the United States. Service self-interest, along with a careful assessment of the military realities, soon forged strong links between both the RCN and the RCAF and their US counterparts.

Only the army hesitated. When Ottawa dispatched a brigade group to Korea in 1950–51, it served in a British-led division and most of its weaponry followed the British pattern. The same held true with the brigade group sent to Germany in 1951. It formed part of the British Army of the Rhine, and only slowly did US-made equipment get taken aboard. General Maurice Pope wrote in 1962 that the 1920s Canadian Army was closely modelled on that of the United Kingdom and, "to a considerable extent," he added, "it still is today." The army was slow to recognize the new reality of power; the air force and navy led the way.

Most important, Canada, based on its assessment of the threat posed by the USSR, had sent troops overseas to serve with NATO at the beginning of the 1950s. True, the Americans pressed Canada to make the commitments, but Canadians usually forget that Canada was present at every stage of the discussions leading to NATO's creation. Moreover, Canadian officials urged a sometimes reluctant and still-isolationist United States to join the defence organization. Canada's safety, Western Europe's security, and the survival of the democracies of the West were at stake, in Ottawa's assessment of the situation, and Canada needed the United States to be the major player. It became so, and this leadership guaranteed Canadian security. Canadians sometimes chafed under the weight of the obligations they had assumed: the Americans got their teeth into North American and Western European defence and, once committed, they would not let go. Nor did they want Canada to do less than it had been doing.

In late 1962 or early 1963 I was a young lieutenant, twenty-three years old and eighteen months out of the Royal Military College, stationed at Camp Borden. My task for one week on the night shift was to be the duty officer at the nuclear warning centre, located on the base, and responsible for warning central Canada of any Soviet attack. It was a few months after the Cuban missile crisis had nearly brought the globe into a third world war (when the warning centre presumably would have been staffed by someone more responsible than Lieutenant Granatstein), but, in the aftermath, the duty was simply boring, ticking off boxes on forms at set times and doing whatever the sergeant in charge told me to do. Nuclear war was a live possibility, and Canada took that possibility seriously. Why else did Prime Minister Diefenbaker want me on duty in the middle of the night?

When the Progressive Conservative Party won its minority victory in the June 1957 election, Canadians were astonished at what they had done. The Liberals had governed for twenty-two years and seemed unbeatable, and almost no one had predicted that the St. Laurent government would be rejected. Diefenbaker, the Saskatchewan lawyer and seventeen-year veteran of Parliament, was just as amazed at the result as the electors.

The new Prime Minister had served in the Canadian Expeditionary Force as a junior officer in the First World War, but his military career ended ingloriously in England when a nervous breakdown seems to have led to his repatriation. During the Second World War, however, like many other Tories, he had called loudly for conscription, and in 1949 he supported joining NATO and, the following year, sending troops to Korea. When he came to power, Diefenbaker believed himself to be a nationalist, a proud defender of the Queen and the Commonwealth, and a stout soldier in the Cold War against the Soviet Union. But he was no military expert. Perhaps that was why he named Major-General George R. Pearkes, a Victoria Cross winner during the Great War and a division commander in Britain in the early years of the Second World War, as his Defence Minister.

Initially Diefenbaker exulted in the thought that he could deal directly with President Dwight Eisenhower, the victorious Allied commander of the Second World War and the President of the United States. He was flattered when "Ike" called him John, sent him notes on important anniversaries, and appeared to listen to what he had to say at their infrequent meetings. Such attentions boosted his sometimes fragile ego, always attuned to slights, real or imagined.

The military relationship between Canada and the United

States had been close since 1940. The two countries had cooperated on a wide range of issues, and American soldiers had built the Alaska Highway through Canada, extracted oil from wells in the North, and flown aircraft over Canadian airspace. As the number of Yanks serving in Edmonton increased, the joke was told, locally, that the telephone at US headquarters was answered with the words "Army of Occupation. How can I help you?" The coming of the Cold War ensured that the Permanent Joint Board of Defence truly became permanent. Once Canada, responding to American pressure, sent troops to Korea and to Western Europe for service under NATO, the military and political alliance between the North American democracies seemed firm.

But beneath the surface of bonhomie, resentments were bubbling. The Americans always pressed Canada to spend more on defence, and sometimes they pushed hard enough to foster hurt feelings in Ottawa. When the Distant Early Warning (DEW) Line was being built in the far North in the mid- to late-1950s to track Soviet bombers that might target US and Canadian cities, American contractors kept out Canadian visitors, including Members of Parliament, though the radar sites were on Canadian soil. That rankled in Ottawa and raised concerns for sovereignty. The Tories in opposition had shouted at the government about that slight. Now they were in power.

The first real test for Diefenbaker came just days after he

45

took office in the summer of 1957. The chairman of the Chiefs of Staff Committee, General Charles Foulkes, saw Pearkes on urgent business. Under the previous government, Foulkes told his Minister, an agreement to create a joint Canada–US air defence command had been negotiated, and the deal was ready for signature when the election was called. The Americans were anxious to proceed. Pearkes acknowledged the urgency—the Soviet bomber threat was real—and he went to see the new Prime Minister. In a few moments the deal was done. Diefenbaker, too, saw the logic and importance of the arrangement, and NORAD, the North American Air Defence Command, came into existence.

Under the agreement, the air defences of Canada and the United States, the fighter squadrons based in both countries, and the radar lines that monitored air traffic coming in over the North Pole were integrated under a joint command, directed from Colorado Springs, Colorado. There a Canadian Air Marshal, C.R. Slemon, sat at the right hand of a US Air Force General as his deputy. Canada had a real share in directing operations, influence in making all policy that affected continental air defence, access to US strategic intelligence, and a genuine role to play not only in its own defence but in that of the United States as well.

The difficulties soon began. Before agreeing to the establishment of the air defence agreement, Pearkes and Diefenbaker had not thought to talk to the Department of

External Affairs, which quickly put forward a host of objections. When Parliament met, the Liberals, who knew what the NORAD file contained, roasted the government for its haste. And when Diefenbaker spoke at a NATO Council meeting later in the year, he argued that NORAD was merely a North American extension of the broader Western alliance. It wasn't true—the Americans adamantly refused to give NATO any say in North America's defence—but what did that matter?

Diefenbaker quickly learned that the subject of defence was a minefield, but he kept running deeper into contested terrain. The Liberals had financed the development of a supersonic fighter, the CF-105 Avro Arrow, but the research and production costs kept escalating at the same time as intercontinental ballistic missiles began to join the superpower arsenals. There seems no reason to doubt that the design work on the interceptor was superb. As it came off the drawing boards, the Arrow was simply beautiful: a big swept-wing aircraft, 14 feet high, 77 feet long, and 50 feet at its widest, it appeared to be a quantum leap ahead of the clunky fighters of the day. The Royal Canadian Air Force estimated that it needed 600 aircraft to defend Canada, but, cautiously, it committed only $27 million in 1953 to develop two prototypes. The Soviet Union soon made its own great advance in long-range bomber design, however, and Ottawa put in more money for eleven prototypes and a pre-production order of twenty-nine aircraft. Then problems arose with the engine intended for the aircraft, and the government agreed reluctantly to invest $70 million in developing a Canadian-designed power plant for the fighter.

Did it make sense to sink hundreds of millions of dollars into this program? At this point, some members of Louis St. Laurent's Liberal government began to wonder if the Arrow shouldn't be cancelled. But the RCAF said that the American and European aircraft under development did not meet Canadian requirements for a long-range fighter, and the decision was reluctantly taken to press on. Soon the Arrow's proposed US weapons system was scrapped, and Canada had to find a replacement. Then the fire-control system also had to be designed from scratch. The costs kept going up, reaching a horrifying $12 million per aircraft at a time when roughly similar American fighters cost about $250,000, thanks to longer production runs and export sales. A small country like Canada simply could not sustain the research, development, and production of a major weapons system. The St. Laurent government likely would have pulled the plug on the Arrow unless the US Air Force or NATO allies bought the fighter, and despite Canada's best efforts, none of them would. The Liberals were now gone, and the US Air Force had its own domestic aircraft makers to satisfy. Shooting down the Arrow fell to the Tories. Screwing up his courage,

Diefenbaker cancelled the contract in February 1959 and ordered that the prototypes be destroyed.

It was the right decision, but clumsily handled, and it has fed discontent among Canada's nationalists and anti-American conspiracy theorists for close to half a century. Today, there are almost a thousand Web sites devoted to the Arrow and several societies that collect Arrow lore. One group is trying to build a full-scale flying Arrow, and another hopes to construct a scaled-down flyable replica. Arrow scrapbooks and a host of books have been published, and a play and a TV docudrama performed. The few parts that survived the wreckers are reverently displayed in museums. The market is apparently endless—and, according to Arrow aficionados, it was all a great US plot to destroy a superb Canadian aircraft.

The CF-105, or so we are told, could have shot down super-secret, high-flying U-2 spy aircraft. But why would Canada want to shoot down American U-2s? Others suggest the Arrow had to be scrapped because the Avro factory had a Soviet mole at work who, when US technology was required for the Arrow, could have passed the Pentagon's secrets to Moscow. But the engine and the weapons system were to be Canadian designed, so what vital US secrets were left—even if there was a spy at the Downsview plant? Or perhaps Diefenbaker cancelled Arrow's production because he was not as nationalist as he claimed, hated Toronto (where the Avro factory was located), or was sold a bill of goods by General Foulkes. Even worse, others suggest with more truth and palpable anti-Americanism bubbling forth, Diefenbaker's closure of the Arrow led to a wholesale brain drain of aircraft specialists to the States, where, working for NASA, they gave the Americans their edge in space. Maybe Canada could have been first on the moon if it weren't for Diefenbaker!

Some fantasists have even suggested that the Arrow could still have been flying today, so advanced was its design. With the Canadian Forces still flying mid-1960s Sea King helicopters and Hercules transports in 2004, of course, that might have come true. That a fighter aircraft, a weapon of war, could stir such passion in our disarmed and pacifistic Canada is surely remarkable. What it suggests is that anti-Americanism (well mixed with prideful nationalism) remains so powerful it can make a fighter aircraft into a Canadian icon.

Canada has a long history—since decades before the Arrow—of arming its forces with weaponry designed more for political purposes than the battlefield. Before the First World War, Canadian soldiers who tested the Ross rifle on the practice range denounced it because it jammed too often. Sam Hughes, the Minister of Militia and Defence, insisted that the Ross be used, and Canadian troops carried it into battle at Ypres—and died in the trenches when it failed in action. In the Second World War, Canada sank millions of dollars into developing the Ram tank, only to scrap it and adopt the American-designed Sherman. In the 1950s the army spent millions more developing an armoured personnel carrier, the Bobcat, only to send it to the junk heap and, in the 1960s, to acquire US-made M-113s, which we continue to use to this day. The navy insisted on building big Tribal Class destroyers in the Second World War, a task beyond Canadian shipyard skills that excelled in constructing corvettes. After the war ended, a few Tribals were built when large sums of cash were poured over all concerned. Diefenbaker showed courage, therefore, in recognizing the realities of mid-twentieth-century life: Canada was a small country with limited resources, and no single weapons system could be allowed to swallow all the available resources.*

From the perspective of history, however, a different announcement by Diefenbaker about defence was far more significant: on February 20, 1959, he told the House of Commons that Canada would accept Bomarc surface-to-air missiles and that the navy and army would have nuclear

51

---

*Resources for the military were already tight and became more so. I can recall training at Camp Borden in 1959–60 in black coveralls rather than summer uniforms and, a year or two later as a young lieutenant, going on exercises in a Jeep without a top—in the pouring rain. Getting a pad or pencil was a major exercise in wheedling.

weapons as well. The Bomarcs, which needed nuclear warheads to be effective, were the government's weapon of
choice to provide the country's air defence contribution to
NORAD. Bases, Diefenbaker continued, would be con-
structed at La Macaza, Quebec, and North Bay, Ontario.
The government would arm the RCAF's CF-104 fighters in
NATO with nuclear warheads for a strike-reconnaissance
role,* provide the army brigade group in NATO with
Honest John short-range surface-to-surface nuclear-tipped
missiles, and give the navy nuclear depth charges. Because of
the "almost unbelievable nature of the world in which we
live," Diefenbaker promised to maintain his government's
contribution to NATO to help the alliance do its job. He had
carried Canada's military into the nuclear age, and the
weapons and their warheads would be in service within a
few years.

If Canadians thought the United States had no reason to
complain, they miscalculated. The neighbours to the south
saw a growing mood of anti-Americanism in Canada and its
government, and they were concerned. An air defence exercise called "Sky Hawk," scheduled for October 1959, first
raised the issue to importance in Washington. After months

---

*Canada acquired 239 CF-104s in all. Over the course of the air-
craft's lifespan in service, some 110 were lost to accidents, earning
the CF-104 the nickname of "Widow-maker" in the air force.

of joint planning, arrangements had been made for civilian air traffic to be grounded to allow USAF bombers to stage a mock attack on NORAD's air defences. Then, suddenly in August, the Diefenbaker Cabinet announced that the exercise was inappropriate and refused to let it proceed. The angry Americans decided that Diefenbaker was capricious, touchy about the wrong things, and not to be relied on to handle military questions sensibly.

Matters did not come to a head, however, until John F. Kennedy entered the White House in January 1961. Kennedy quickly discovered that he had little time for "Deefenbawker," as he mispronounced the Prime Minister's name at their first meeting. The sententious older man bored the vigorous new President, and Kennedy make no secret of his view that Canada should get its act together and do more in the Cold War. Yearning for the respectful treatment he had almost always received from Eisenhower, Diefenbaker was soon set to explode.

The issue was Cuba, where Fidel Castro had seized power, set up a communist state, and proceeded to execute or exile his enemies. The Soviet Union, delighted to have an ally off the coast of Florida, provided aid and oil in large quantities, and the furious Kennedy Administration schemed and plotted the overthrow of Castro and imposed a trade boycott. Canada piously urged moderation on the United States and, at the same time, tried to increase its trade with Cuba at

53

American expense. This attitude did not go over well in the United States, where it was seen as perverse anti-Americanism. Then, in October 1962, American U-2 spy planes found proof that the Soviet Union had secretly begun to construct intermediate-range ballistic missile bases on the island. These missiles could easily strike American targets, and, with nuclear warheads, the damage they might cause was incalculable.

The Cuban crisis now escalated dramatically and threatened to cause an all-out nuclear war. Surely Canada would stand by its superpower ally in this greatest crisis of the Cold War? The Americans had few doubts when they sent their former Ambassador to Canada, Livingston Merchant, to show the Prime Minister in Ottawa the photographs of the missile sites a few hours before Kennedy went on television to speak to the world. Diefenbaker nodded, appeared to understand, and the envoy departed for Washington.

As soon as the President's address ended, NORAD went to DEFCON 3, the mid-point of the five alert statuses, indicating serious international tension. At Colorado Springs the joint air staff anticipated that the RCAF's fighter squadrons in NORAD would go on alert at once. No order was forthcoming, however, and Douglas Harkness, who had replaced General Pearkes as Defence Minister in 1960, went to see the Prime Minister. To his utter astonishment he found that Diefenbaker would not give the order. The Cabinet had to decide, Diefenbaker said, his anger at President Kennedy spilling over into policy matters. If the United States were treating Canada as a true partner, the Prime Minister clearly believed, word on the Soviet missiles in Cuba would have been given days and not just hours before Kennedy spoke on TV. The photographs of the bases under construction clearly had not impressed Diefenbaker.

The next morning Harkness explained to his Cabinet colleagues why the alert was necessary. The Russians were building missile bases that could strike US targets, Soviet ships carrying more missiles were en route to Cuba, and Kennedy had ordered the US Navy to intercept them and to impose a blockade on Cuba. War, a nuclear war, was a very real possibility. Many of the ministers, led by their chief, refused to accept Harkness's arguments. Why should the Americans be believed? Wasn't the Kennedy Administration pushy, aggressive, and unreliable? Moreover, an alert would alarm the country, Diefenbaker said, and "we should wait and see what happened." As political commentator James Eayrs put it, perhaps Diefenbaker's position was based on the idea of "no annihilation without representation." Nothing else made much sense.

Harkness returned to his office and quietly gave orders that the Canadian forces should go on alert "without putting the country in turmoil," despite the Cabinet's refusal to authorize it. CF-101 Voodoo fighter jets armed up—without nuclear weapons because Canada had not yet agreed to accept them—and went to standby status on their runways. The army quietly called soldiers on leave back to their bases. Some ships had already put to sea from Halifax, relieving US Navy ships tracking Soviet submarines, while others steamed in for replenishment and a quick turnaround. "The navy," wrote Commander Tony German, "honoured Canada's duty to stand by [its] North American ally," even if the government did not. The admirals commanding on the east and west coasts did what they believed necessary and followed their orders in the "RCN Defence Plan." The military was now on alert—in defiance of the Prime Minister.

In Parliament, Diefenbaker called on the United Nations to investigate the situation in Cuba. In effect he was suggesting that Kennedy had lied about the presence of Soviet missiles there and that he questioned the photographic evidence he had been shown. That infuriated the White House, as did the continuing delay in putting NORAD on alert. On October 24, with NORAD now on DEFCON 2, a very high state of readiness, Harkness finally pressed a reluctant Diefenbaker to agree that the Canadian fighter squadrons could go on alert. "All right," the Prime Minister said, scowling, "go ahead." "I never told him," Harkness said later, "that I had already done so."

The Kennedy Administration found its way out of the crisis, and the Soviet Union removed the missiles from Cuba.

The greatest confrontation of the Cold War had ended without bloodshed, but there was no doubt that Canada had failed to meet its obligations. The Americans knew, the Canadian Cabinet knew, and soon the Canadian public knew it too. When the media began to report that Diefenbaker had delayed in putting RCAF squadrons in NORAD on alert, the public was outraged. It was one thing to pull tail feathers from the American eagle in peacetime; it was another, entirely, to posture in a crisis that threatened Canada's cities with nuclear devastation as much as it did US urban areas. Even Tory stalwarts lost faith in Diefenbaker, a leader whose political position had been in doubt ever since the June 1962 election gave him a minority government. "We were not a satellite state," Diefenbaker grumpily wrote in his memoirs, "at the beck and call of an imperial master." Absolutely true, but there are times when allies must come when called. The Cuban missile crisis was one of them.

After the Cuban crisis, not only the Americans but the opposition, the media, and some Conservatives in both the Cabinet and the party all wanted Diefenbaker's head. So, too, did the Canadian military, as the RCAF in particular ran a quiet campaign to brief Canadian media and business elites on the ways in which Canada had failed to meet its commitments. The Canadian military, wrote political scientist Jocelyn Ghent, "perceived and acted on a threat that was defined not by their government, but by the transgovernmental group to which they felt much closer, the Canadian-American military." Such action was grossly improper, a complete failure in civil-military relations; but it was completely understandable in light of the threat to Canada and North America. The military saw the dangers even if the government did not.

The opportunity to get rid of the Prime Minister was soon at hand. The Bomarc missile bases were almost ready, and Canada had yet to strike an arrangement with the United States to resolve the matter of custody of the nuclear war-heads. US law required that nuclear warheads remain in American custody until, in a crisis, they could be released. In effect, there was a two-key system—one key held by a US officer, the other by a Canadian. Both keys, with both countries in agreement, had to be turned at the same time.

The difficulties in Ottawa lay in a struggle between the Department of External Affairs and the Department of National Defence. The military argued that Canada had committed itself to take the warhead. Everything else was house-keeping. The striped-pants brigade maintained that there was no real commitment and that Canada should not accept the warheads as long as there was any prospect of a nuclear disarmament treaty between the great powers. In the middle hovered Diefenbaker, talking to his neutralist and anti-American External Affairs Minister, Howard Green; pondering the anti-American broadcasts of James M. Minifie, the CBC's Washington correspondent; and reading his mail each day from Voice of Women branches and other peace activists. One week he seemed willing to move ahead, but the next his doubts returned and he hung back. With the two Bomarc bases ready, he had to decide on the nuclear warheads, but he simply could not. Frustrated beyond endurance and eager to hit at the Prime Minister, the US State Department issued a press release on January 30, 1963, stating bluntly that "the Canadian Government has not as yet proposed any arrangement sufficiently practical to contribute effectively to North American defence." The US Ambassador in Ottawa, Walton W. Butterworth, wrote that it would be "very useful" and "highly beneficial in advancing U.S. interests by introducing realism into a government which had made anti-Americanism and indecision practically its entire stock-in-trade." Privately, he said, "We had to set the record straight. . . . If you want to play rough, then we'll play rough too. They chose the weapon."

The press release proved explosive. Within days the government lost a vote of confidence in Parliament, the Cabinet fell apart, and Diefenbaker had to call an election. He was a dead political duck, or so everyone believed. Instead, the Chief fought a magnificent, unscrupulous, and effective anti-American campaign, attacking Kennedy, the United States, the Pentagon, the worth of the Bomarcs, and the Liberals as Yankee puppets. It was a shameful display, but Diefenbaker, his party in ruins, almost pulled it off. The Liberals won power with only a minority government.

59

The lesson was obvious: anti-Americanism still worked in Canada. It made no difference that Diefenbaker had let down his neighbour by failing to put NORAD, the defensive alliance he himself had signed, on alert in the greatest crisis of the Cold War. It made no difference that Diefenbaker had balked at accepting the nuclear warheads needed to make effective the Bomarcs he himself had acquired from the United States. A large percentage of the Canadian people let themselves be gulled by anti-Americanism and fooled by a political leader whose main weapon was shamelessness.

Diefenbaker had made the fundamental error that Canadian politicians, media, and far too many citizens still make today. He believed he could do anything—or not do something the situation demanded—and the United States would never react against Canada, its best friend. He was wrong. On security issues, on matters where they believed their national survival was at stake, the Americans were prepared to do whatever they had to do. Canadians today who worry that the United States is overreacting to the terrorist threat would do well to remember this example. The Cuban missile crisis had demonstrated to Washington that war was a real possibility, and North American defences had to be prepared. Canada had to pull its weight. As it turned out, all it took to finish Diefenbaker off in Cabinet and in Parliament, to knock him from the prime ministerial perch, was a simple, blunt State Department press release. The Chief had badly miscalculated.

In yet another fundamental mistake, Diefenbaker had also believed that Canada's sovereignty could only be enhanced or preserved by saying no to the Americans, breaking long-standing obligations, being difficult, and perpetually playing the sulking little brother. In fact, all actions of this sort do is threaten the manifold economic and personal links across the border on which Canada's economy depends. In the missile crisis of 1962, Diefenbaker's inaction threatened Canadian and US security, and the United States, far more committed to winning the Cold War than was Canada, simply could not allow that to happen. Had the worst occurred in October 1962, the United States would have sent its fighter aircraft into Canada and its bombers over Canadian territory to attack the USSR, whatever Canada's government said, because it had to do what was necessary to prevail and to survive. Perhaps Canada might also have survived a nuclear war; if it did, it would not have been because of its government's actions.

Sovereignty is exercised by acting in the national interest, by behaving as a mature nation, and by meeting the treaty obligations Canadian governments has freely entered. In October 1962 a sensible government would have accepted the US evidence of Soviet missile bases in Cuba, first because the evidence was correct, and second because the United States, a longstanding ally, could be trusted. The government should not have called on the United Nations to investigate,

an action that played into Soviet hands by suggesting dis-
belief. It ought to have authorized its forces to go on alert
immediately, and it ought to have supported the United States
diplomatically, politically, and militarily. That is the way
allies behave; in particular, it is the way friends act in a crisis.
Even France under Charles de Gaulle, who was far more suspicious of the United States than Diefenbaker, gave unstinting
support in the Cuban crisis. For Canada, a small nation abut-
ting a superpower, that is simply the way we must behave in
our own national interests. That the Americans were right in
Cuba, that the USSR had endangered the world in putting
missiles there, simply made Diefenbaker's utterly foolish position all the more incomprehensible.

The Americans, clearly relieved that Diefenbaker was out
of office by April 1963, never quite trusted Canada again.
They had seen that anti-Americanism could trump common
sense, that some Canadians in and near power were, if anything, more suspicious of Washington than of Moscow. Little
that happened after 1962–63 would force them to change
their minds, because the calculus of anti-Americanism as a
tool of governance in Canada had become a self-fulfilling
prophecy. Canadian governments loved to crow about sovereignty or to proclaim their independence, and prime ministers and Cabinet ministers deliberately encouraged
quasi-neutralist thinking in the population. To be fair, however, the United States did sometimes tramp around the

world in hobnailed boots, its reach ranging from Southeast Asia to the Arctic and to the Middle East. But leaders have a duty to separate what is important from what is not, and Canada's elites didn't make the effort to do so.

The Vietnam War preoccupied the United States from the early 1960s until the fall of Saigon and the communists' victory a decade later. The Americans pressed their friends for support, but Lester Pearson's Liberal government declined. The commitment to the International Control Commission, nominally supervising the "truce" in Vietnam, forbade the country from taking sides—or so Ottawa argued. This was a logical and defensible position, and Canada served US interests during the war by carrying messages from Washington to Hanoi and by some discreet information-gathering in North Vietnam. Pearson, however, won no friends by making a speech in Philadelphia denouncing the American bombings of Hanoi. It was one thing to protest US policy; it was another to do so on US soil. President Lyndon Johnson, with some justification, was furious as he declared that Pearson had "pissed on his rug."

Diefenbaker had poisoned the well. He played to Canadians' nationalism—which always translated into anti-Americanism—and he spread the infection deep into the bone of the Liberal Party too. No one doubted that Canada was an independent and sovereign nation, able to plot its own course, but its leaders had made choices extending back to the Kingston and Woodbridge speeches of 1938, the Ogdensburg Agreement of August 1940, the NORAD agreement of 1957–58, and a host of others. They had done so because they recognized quite properly that Canada needed the military protection the United States could offer. In return, Canadian governments agreed to maintain the defence of their territory at a level sufficient to ensure that the United States would not be exposed to danger because of Canadian weakness. It was a bargain between sovereign states, each contributing what it could to their joint defence. Helping to bring the United States aboard, Canada joined NATO in 1949, with all but unanimous support in Parliament, because the government recognized that the defence of democracy in Western Europe was as important as in North America. Had Canada not paid its full measure in blood for that principle in the two world wars?

Somehow, Canadians drifted away from good sense in their military relations with the United States. It began with John Diefenbaker, one of the killers of the Canadian military, and his example of virulent anti-Americanism still inspires his successors. It is long past time for Canadians to begin to act in their true national interest. Above all, that means cooperating closely with our neighbours in the defence of North America. In real terms, Canada has no choice here, though it can exercise its independent judgment when the United States goes to war abroad. Even then, our leaders need to weigh the risk of alienating the United States against the national interest in advancing global freedom and democracy and in keeping dollars, trade, and people moving across the border. This is a neat balancing act, but getting it right is a test of prime ministerial greatness. John Diefenbaker—and Jean Chrétien after him—got it hopelessly wrong.

CHAPTER 3

Trial by Error: Paul Hellyer and the Unification of the Forces

WHO killed the Canadian military? Paul Hellyer, the Minister of National Defence who, in the 1960s, first integrated and then unified the Canadian Armed Forces. Ambitious, tough, intelligent, Hellyer picked up the army, navy, and air force, shook them vigorously, and rearranged the Canadian military into a new, strange form. In the process, some things were gained, but much was lost.

Paul Hellyer is a complex, maddening, revolutionary figure. Born in Waterford, Ontario, in 1923, he joined the Royal Canadian Air Force in the spring of 1944 and began training to become a pilot. But late in 1944 the RCAF decided it had too many surplus aircrew, so it released Hellyer after a nine-week process of administrative confusion. Then and later, it would strike Hellyer as absurdly bad planning that his release came at the same time that the army overseas was hit by a grave shortage of infantry reinforcements, a crisis so severe it would force the Mackenzie King government to send home-defence conscripts to fight in Europe.

Hellyer joined the army as soon as he could, only compounding his unhappiness. "I received new documentation and new 'dog tags,'" he wrote. "Then there was drill. When I mentioned that I was fully trained in the art of forming threes, I was told 'that was air force square-bashing.' Next was gas drill," very much the same, and a series of painful immunization shots to add to those the RCAF had given him. As Hellyer said, he resented this administrivia at a time when the army overseas was in difficulty for want of soldiers. "Grown men indulged in silly games that squandered valuable time. There was little effective cooperation between the services when each concentrated almost exclusively on its own interests." He was absolutely correct, though he never quite understood that army training and discipline aimed to prepare men to work together in large numbers under fire. Aircrew training, in contrast, was more individualistic. The services shared many similarities—a vaccination was a vaccination was a sore arm—but there were also real differences. Hellyer never grasped the distinctions—and that caused difficulties two decades later.

Others had recognized the problems of service triplication during and after the war. Brooke Claxton was Defence Minister for Prime Ministers Mackenzie King and Louis St. Laurent from 1946 to 1954, and he ran the three services under a single ministry; during the Second World War, however, there had been different ministers for each one. Claxton created the post of Chairman of the Chiefs of Staff Committee and gave it first to General Charles Foulkes, a wartime corps commander and Canada's pre-eminent military bureaucrat. The Chairman's job was to try to impose coordination on the services and to give the Minister advice on how Canada could have a single defence policy. Claxton also reopened the Royal Military College in Kingston, Ontario, as a tri-service institution and began the unification of the military's padres and the legal, dental, and medical services, with one of the armed services operating the specific function for the other two. Under John Diefenbaker's first Defence Minister, General George Pearkes, the process of coordination continued, as the procurement of food and postal services became tri-service. The easy bits had been joined together, but there the process stalled.

By this time, Paul Hellyer had become a successful property developer and was in politics. He first won election to Parliament as a twenty-six-year-old Liberal in a downtown Toronto riding in 1949 and was re-elected in 1953. Just before the 1957 election, Prime Minister St. Laurent put him in the Cabinet as Associate Minister of National Defence, the first Liberal Cabinet minister from Toronto ever (or so Hellyer said), but his time in the ministry was brief. Both Hellyer and the Liberals went down to defeat in June 1957. In the huge Diefenbaker sweep of 1958 Hellyer lost again, but he won a by-election later that year and soon became a key shaper of the Liberals' defence policy in opposition. When he visited the Canadian forces in NATO, he became convinced, correctly, that under the Diefenbaker government Canada was not meeting its nuclear commitments to the alliance. He had seen the RCAF in NATO in 1955 and found the pilots happy "because their souped-up F-86 Sabre aircraft could fly rings around the Americans. Now," he discovered in 1962, "the government was refusing to arm the F-104s it had purchased [with nuclear weapons] . . . and pilots were so ashamed they avoided bars frequented by their NATO colleagues." The army was in similarly bad shape, its troops without armoured personnel carriers, its Honest John missile warheads filled with sand.

As much as any man, Hellyer was responsible for persuading Lester Pearson to reverse his party's position and to come out in favour of Canada's acceptance of the nuclear weapons Diefenbaker had agreed to acquire. When Pearson won the April 1963 general election, he made Hellyer his Defence Minister.

The armed forces Hellyer found numbered 123,000 regulars, who operated on a defence budget of $1.73 billion (or $8.2 billion in constant 1992–93 dollars), a budget that had declined substantially since the Liberals were last in office. Worse, only 13.6 percent of the budget went to equipment, half of what was required to renew the forces' capital stock. (Ten years before, 42.9 percent of the budget had been spent on equipment.) Each service had its own tasks and war plans, and none was geared to support the others in war. The service chiefs competed with each other for funds, while the Chairman of the Chiefs of Staff Committee vainly tried to referee. Committees piled atop committees, and triplication of functions was common. "A cascade of committees," retired Major-General W.H.S. Macklin called it, with the Chairman's job "a phony substitute for unity." Hellyer saw nothing but open competition among the services and constant political manoeuvring, as each service chief exercised his right of direct access to the Minister. It made no rational sense, he decided, and he set out to fix matters.

In a White Paper released in 1964, Hellyer laid out his plans. He wanted to integrate the forces under a single Chief of the Defence Staff and an integrated Defence Staff at a renamed Canadian Forces Headquarters. The Chiefs of the General Staff, Naval Staff, and Air Staff would be eliminated. This reorganization, Hellyer said, could enhance civilian control of the military and save money by avoiding wasteful triplication. His goal was to double the capital account and re-equip the brigades in Canada. The main roles of the military would remain service in NATO, NORAD, and UN peacekeeping, and Hellyer proposed to add a mobile force with the capacity to operate anywhere. This US Marine Corps clone could have its own ships, aircraft, and infantry—and Hellyer launched a process that bought F-5 tactical ground support fighters for this force, even though, he said later, this aircraft was "little more than a trainer with guns hung on it." For the first time, a part of Canada's armed forces would be able to fight together on land, at sea, and in the air. The White Paper added, in one sentence, that integration "is the first step toward a single unified service for Canada." Hellyer thought that statement was the most he could get the service chiefs and the Chairman of the Chiefs of Staff Committee to swallow.

Certainly, the military chiefs were not entirely happy with integration—the Chief of the Air Staff "apprehensive" and the Chief of Naval Staff "very much so," Hellyer recalled—but neither were they alarmed. New Defence Ministers usually had their own ideas, but the system and the weight of tradition always broke them down, "civilized" (or, in this case, "militarized") them, and made them amenable to reason. But not Hellyer. In late 1964 he told the generals there would be a single recruiting system, a common basic training organization and trades training system, and full integration at headquarters and in the field. "I suggested that officers should get enthusiastic about integration," Hellyer wrote later, "or else turn in their badges and take the special benefits available to them." To get the money for new equipment, he announced a cut of 10,000 men, an arbitrary 20-percent reduction of the 50,000 personnel employed in support roles. Ottawa headquarters was to be slashed by 30 percent.

No one in the military was pleased, but the changes of integration had not yet reached the level of true pain, despite the administrative confusion they caused at headquarters in Ottawa. ("If my boss calls while I'm out," colonels told their secretaries as jobs and organization charts changed daily, "get his name.") The public relations functions of the three services quickly and easily combined into one, as did construction engineering, communications, and intelligence. A single comptroller-general and a common pay system made sense; a uniform personnel system could be justified; and a common logistics system and technical services branch were potentially helpful if they could be made to take account of the different requirements of the navy, air force, and army. Some doubted strongly they could, though fairness compelled them to recognize that savings in dollars, personnel, and time could be realized.

With everyone in the military already suffering from "integration neurosis," the hard part now began. In mid-1965 Hellyer shoehorned the three services' eleven commands into six functional organizations: Mobile Command, which encompassed the army and tactical air support; Maritime Command, bringing together the navy and anti-submarine aircraft; Air Defence Command; Air Transport Command; Training Command; and Material Command. For a period, nothing worked properly, as units and personnel were shuffled into place. The brigade and the fighter-bomber squadrons in NATO were not formally part of this homeland structure and their efficiency was not directly affected, though officers and men were every bit as nervous as their peers at home as change rolled on.

Tough and shrewd, often even sly, Hellyer paid no attention to the fearful and the doubters as he relentlessly pressed ahead. Soon, generals, air marshals, and admirals began to retire—in droves. Between January 1965 and August 1966, twenty-eight general officers departed, including three of the "three stars" (lieutenant-generals or their equivalents), and seventy-nine senior officers in all. Thousands of other officers and senior non-commissioned ranks, 26,300 in the period since Hellyer took office, also left (one of them being Lieutenant Granatstein). Officers had to be promoted to fill the vacated positions—in August 1966 only two of the thirteen most senior officers had been in their commands for more than a month—and those who did rise to higher rank had many different motives. Some agreed with unification and moved up the ladder cheerfully; some were trimmers who supported anything that would get them promotion; some recognized they owed their men loyalty and could protect them best if they had a higher rank; and some aimed to secure changes they had long sought.

The new Chief of the Defence Staff (CDS), General Jean-Victor Allard, was one of those who wanted change. Hellyer appointed him in June 1966 after he had served as the first commander of Mobile Command. The Minister liked the General's ebullience and the idea of appointing a francophone to the top job, correctly believing that Allard would prove more amenable to his wishes than other candidates for CDS. As a French Canadian, Allard's devotion to the British-style traditions of the forces was probably less strong, and he was certainly less enamoured of the "royal" nomenclature that pervaded the military. To Hellyer, this quality was important because Pearson, after being embarrassed by the difficulties of getting Canada into the UN Emergency Force in 1956, was believed to be keen on "Canadianizing" the country. A different and distinctive military, like a new flag, might appeal to the Prime Minister, and Hellyer knew he would need Pearson's support.

Allard quickly seized his chance to press bilingualism on the Canadian Forces, a long-sought personal goal. This request also helped Hellyer with the Cabinet, because the question of Quebec's place in Canada was increasingly to the fore. Bilingualism was a worthwhile and necessary goal, but, amid the rapid and radical changes of unification, it only increased fear and despondency in the military.

In December 1965 the Minister called his senior officers together for a meeting and laid out his plan for a unified force with a collective name and a common rank structure. Did he mean to make "universalists?" he was asked—a tank driver flying a helicopter and firing a destroyer's guns in a

77

single week. Of course not, he replied. "The forces will always require technically trained specialists to undertake specialist missions on land, sea, and air and there should be no apprehension about this." What was involved, Hellyer said, was determining "whether this can best be accomplished with forces as separate legal entities and with separate identities or as one unified force." But what about tradition, or regimental and service identity? The generals and admirals raised the questions, but Hellyer dismissed such things as "buttons and bows." The traditions of the services meant little to the Minister. Yet to senior officers who had watched men fight and die for their regiments, ships, and squadrons, the names of units and corps and the peculiar, particular traditions of the services had real meaning. Moreover, careers and promotions were at stake, and there were a million Great War and Second World War veterans in the population, most of whom had attachments to their service and unit traditions. Yet, in Hellyer's interpretation, "there was no valid military objection to unification" at the meeting. "The opposition was purely emotional."

It was a very emotional, and angry, navy that led the charge. The smallest of the services, the most traditional, and historically the most inhospitable to francophones, the Royal Canadian Navy also had a keen sense of itself, good leadership, and an ethical tradition that encouraged senior officers to speak their minds. Nelson had held a telescope to his blind

78

eye when there were signals he did not want to see. He had also led his men into the fight and was ready to die gloriously. His 1960s Canadian counterpart was Rear-Admiral William Landymore, commanding on the Atlantic coast. In addresses to his sailors and in testimony to a parliamentary committee in mid-1966, the Admiral left no doubt that he thought unification would destroy the RCN and its effectiveness. When Hellyer sacked him, Landymore carried his fight to the media, telling the press that unification had demoralized the officer corps. In return, an exasperated Hellyer said the Admiral had been fired for "18 months consistent disloyalty to the policy of the people he was paid to serve," a charge he subsequently withdrew. Disloyalty? For trying to save the navy as he knew it? For resisting a Minister who believed he could stand the military world on its head?

Landymore and the other officers who resisted unification did so in ways that fit within the rules of Canadian civil-military relations. They avoided the defiance exhibited in the 1962 Cuban missile crisis, when the Royal Canadian Navy put to sea without government orders to work with its United States Navy ally. During the unification debate, the generals and admirals raised their objections to the Minister's policy in private; they tried to persuade him to change his mind; and when they failed, they resigned or, in a few cases, were fired. But disloyalty was never the issue, and Hellyer erred grievously in charging Landymore with that

79

gross military crime. The senior officers acted properly. So too did Hellyer—as a Minister he had every right to press his and his government's chosen policy forward. If he wanted "one force with a common name, a common uniform and common rank designations," he had every constitutional right to try to get it.

Landymore's sacking galvanized the battle over Hellyer's plans. Soon anti-unification organizations were formed by reservists, veterans, and others, the most important being TRIO, the Tri-Service Identities Organization. They had much media support and many backers in the House of Commons. At this time, twenty years after V-E Day, there were still many MPs who had served during the war (and even a few who had fought in the Great War). Compared with 2004, when the list of MPs with any military service can be counted on the fingers of one hand, Parliament was relatively knowledgeable about the armed forces. So, too, was the electorate. Still, defence was not high on the political agenda, and one observer suggested cynically that "90 percent of the Cabinet didn't know the difference between NORAD and NATO." If that was true of ministers, how much more so of ordinary MPs and Canadians generally?

There did seem to be public interest in the debate over unification, however. In late 1966, the first year that I taught history at York University after I left the army, I participated in a debate on unification with a distinguished Royal Canadian

Navy reserve officer—a Commodore, in fact. The audience was large and the action heavy. The Commodore opposed unification, and I, in part at least for a lively discussion, supported it. In my memory, I won the debate hands down, perhaps because, in making the point that unification was going to change things, I addressed him throughout as Brigadier-General, the army equivalent of his naval rank that was supposed to become the new Canadian military norm. He was unhappy at my effrontery, but several years later when I was writing a scholarly piece on the unification of the Canadian Forces, he graciously allowed me to use his papers. He showed much more class than I had.

But that didn't save the Commodore or the Royal Canadian Navy. Hellyer had the support of the Prime Minister, somewhat grudgingly, and of his senior Cabinet colleagues. Unification was intended to save money and, to Ministers, less money for defence meant more money for their departments. In the House, the whip was cracked and the MPs jumped, even though filibustered hearings before a parliamentary committee and lengthy debates in the House of Commons were extraordinarily testy. The unification bill, signalling the end of the Royal Canadian Navy, the Royal Canadian Air Force, and the Canadian Army, passed into law in April 1967 and came into effect the next year. The Canadian Forces took their place, unique in the world as members of a unified force. Soon they were wearing a new green uniform, made from the cloth used for gas station attendants—or so Toronto lawyer Michael Levine, the son of the clothing supplier, recollected thirty-five years later.

Was unification a political error and a military mistake? Hellyer had created a policy for a Canadian military that had previously had no common policy. He had integrated the headquarters and made it more efficient, reducing the staff from 12,000 to 8,000. He had slashed committees and put in place a more rational acquisition process for capital equipment, though he had largely failed in getting additional money for new kit. He had envisaged a Canadian military that could fight on the sea, on land, and in the air, each service supporting the other—a truly revolutionary concept for Canada. He had put functional commands in the field, bringing together jealous service empires that had resisted cooperation in the past. He had reduced supply depots from fifteen to four, training camps from eleven to two, and basic officer training bases from three to one. These steps saved millions of dollars. All these changes were useful, necessary, right, and proper. If Hellyer had only stopped there, he would rank as the greatest of Canadian military reformers since Sir Frederick Borden at the beginning of the twentieth century.

82

But Hellyer went that one step too far when he created a unified service wearing a single uniform with a common rank structure. He wanted there to be something above single service loyalty—a loyalty to the Canadian Forces. But loyalty to the navy, army, and air force, to corps and regiments, ships, and squadrons was vital for sailors, soldiers, and airmen and women whose job it was to fight and risk their lives to serve their country's interests. It might be peripheral to the Minister, but it was heritage, tradition, and hard-earned distinctions to fighting men. Sailors in particular revolted at the idea that colonels should command ships and that a green uniform would replace the traditional bell-bottoms. How would that look when they went ashore in Plymouth or New Orleans? Arrogant as he was, Hellyer didn't understand this concern. And his arrogance, his rigidity, seemed obvious to the public and to everyone in government and the media. Paul Hellyer, they knew, would never be prime minister.

His legacy was a unified force supported by the "purple" trades, the trades that were not part of the three "environments"—a new word to describe what used to be the services. In a unified force, an engine artificer previously in the RCN could work at an air force base and fit in, so long as he could master aircraft engines and everyone wore the same green uniform. Too often, however, the level of expertise wasn't there, and the former sailor attached to a logistics unit supporting an army brigade did not know how to survive in the field. "You couldn't have an army cook on a ship," one Admiral recollected. "The cook wouldn't be on the team and couldn't handle other roles." Inevitably, the quality of support for all three environments deteriorated for a time.

Still, the system could have been made to work. Some tweaking here and there, some concessions to the different needs of the environments, some words of assurance—some were, in fact, offered, as when the navy was permitted to keep its own rank structure and even to wear the old-style uniforms aboard ship (if officers and ratings provided them). What made it difficult was the unwillingness of many in the service—and almost everyone who had once been in the military—to accept unification. There were too few like General Jacques Dextraze who, while admitting he had not been happy with unification, recognized that people initially "fight against an idea, lose, and then try to make the new system work."

Complicating everything was the fact that Canada as a whole was entering a difficult period, and the Canadian Forces were already well into their decades of decline. When Pierre Trudeau became Prime Minister in 1968 and froze the defence budget, he put an end to any chances of new equipment. Inflation began to pick up speed and soon bit deeply into this already restricted budget. Bilingualism and the creation of French Language Units shook the Canadian Forces, even as it tried to absorb the shock of unification. The establishment of a common training system weakened tradition, and the closing of regimental officers' and NCOs' messes and their replacement by base messes hurt unit cohesion—even if it cut down excessive drinking at subsidized prices! Bases were consolidated to save money, a useful goal but one that reduced the military "footprint" in the community. The government cut Canada's NATO commitment by half. Most serious of all were the changes at Canadian Forces Headquarters that came into force under Trudeau's government.

Defence Minister Donald C. Macdonald established a Management Review Group in 1971 to study his department. The tradition had been for a civilian deputy minister to handle the money while the uniformed staff directed operations and training. In practice, then, the generals had the operational responsibility but no control over the funds necessary to pay the costs, and a "mini–Treasury Board" in the deputy minister's office had the final say. The Defence Council, where Hellyer had expected the Chief of the Defence Staff to bring everything together, was effectively paralyzed by infighting and all but incapable of moving agreed recommendations forward. Macdonald watched as the Department of National Defence made little headway in presenting its policies and its requests to Cabinet. Was the Department intellectually dead, he wondered, or was its bureaucracy wrongly directed? If so, what could be done to get its management up to speed, to make DND function as well as Britain's Ministry of Defence, where the senior officers appeared to work effectively with career civil servants? Above all, how could he get control of the policy options presented to him? That was the true purpose of the department management review.

The Review Group, headed by businessman John Pennefather of Montreal, recommended that the Deputy Minister should be senior to the Chief of the Defence Staff, a recommendation that the Deputy, Sylvain Cloutier, and the CDS, General Dextraze, soon agreed was wrong. They argued that they should be co-equals, with a combined staff serving both.* The Minister agreed, and an integrated civil-military staff, 10,000 strong, came into being at National Defence Headquarters. Before the changeover in October 1972, the Deputy Minister had a staff of 400, all working to assess and approve the military's requests. But with an integrated civil-military structure, such a staff became unnecessary, as a single unified staff served both the Deputy and the CDS. The system worked, so long as Cloutier and Dextraze were in charge. They fought in private, working out their positions; in public, they presented a unified and common front.

Cloutier put new bureaucrats in place. He appointed an assistant deputy minister for matériel, a new financial

---

*The clarity Cloutier and Dextrase saw may have been less evident to others. Douglas Bland of Queen's University asked one former Minister of National Defence who was on top, the CDS or the DM, or were both equals. "I didn't know and couldn't find out" came the reply.

administrator, and an assistant deputy minister for policy, the last an effort to give the Department of National Defence some clout in dealing with the Department of External Affairs. These were essential changes, but the overall effect of the new organization at National Defence Headquarters was harmful; the former army officer turned professor, Douglas Bland, called the result "institutionalized ambiguity." "Advance and be reorganized" was the way wags put it, but clearly this reorganization was at least as significant as unification in its long-term impact on the Canadian military.

Now civilian officers could outrank military officers who worked for them. Now an Admiral or a General could be styled an Associate Assistant Deputy Minister. Now the military, which ordinarily posted officers to new positions every two or three years, rotated its personnel into and out of Ottawa on a regular basis and saw the long-serving civilians become the repository of memory—and power. Many complained that civilians "tend to provide the continuity and seem to have an undue influence," resulting in "civilian management, rather than civilian control." Bland put it more bluntly: "At best, military officers who attempt to perform on public service terms are considered 'lightweights' in bureaucratic infighting. At worst, in the opinion of a past DM, they are considered to be liabilities who should be excluded from policy positions in NDHQ." The civilians said they knew best how to fight and win Ottawa's wars, and that may well have been true.

What also occurred was the "civilianization" of the military. A large cadre of military managers, neither warriors nor bureaucrats, began to grow and thrive as the Canadian Forces tried desperately to counter the power of the civilians. But to oppose them effectively, it was necessary to be more like them. The day of the officer who was a business school graduate, the day of the hated "bean counters," had arrived, and headquarters assumed ever more control over the operational side of the forces. The civil servants and the NDHQ officers seemed to merge into one group—corporate managers, certainly not military leaders—and the senior officers appeared to forget over time what it had once been like in the field. The military managers and their interests, while ultimately different from those of the civilian bureaucrats, became far removed from the concerns of a fighter squadron commander or a destroyer captain. To both categories of managers, the interests of National Defence Headquarters always seemed more important and more pressing than those of the troops in the field. They were running a big business, after all. They had to seek corporate-style efficiencies to meet the demands of the government, and the demands of the military workforce for change came to be treated with condescension at best and contempt at worst. The status quo was always better than change (which, given the rapid transformations of the Canadian Forces, may have been true) and, in any case, National Defence Headquarters could always outlast everyone else. The civilians would always be there. Over time, the Canadian Forces became captive of a system it could not change—or master.

The military hated this role. A scholarly study by Peter Kasurak in 1982 argued that "a significant number of the members of the armed services have come to believe that the Canadian Forces have adopted civilian norms and standards to an unacceptable degree and that civilian public servants exercise undue influence over matters that are (or should be) exclusively military in nature." Bland echoed this complaint, adding that officers at National Defence Headquarters didn't know to whom they should report—the Deputy Minister or the Chief of the Defence Staff or both. Nor did they know from whom their orders emanated. When advice had to go to the government, who prevailed—the more realistic soldiers or the politically flexible bureaucrats? As Bland observed, the civil servants "can take the long view and are not tied to the soldier's code." In effect, the soldier's ethos of "mission before self" was gradually being diluted by bureaucratic expediency. Some officers worried that successive Chiefs of the Defence Staff appeared to agree with—or at least acquiesce in—this state of affairs.

The system functioned so long as the Deputy Minister of Defence and the Chief of the Defence Staff kept it going, but not all such arrangements could be as harmonious or as successful as the Cloutier-Dextraze marriage had been. With increasing difficulty, the CDS tried to control the "service-driven agendas" of the navy, army, and air force and the other commands, to satisfy the demands of senior officers, and to keep an arduous schedule. The personal diary of one Chief in the late 1980s showed three hundred evening functions in a year, a punishing domestic and international travel schedule, and a daily agenda of committee meetings followed by briefings and more committee meetings. There was little time for thinking. At times the Deputy Minister dominated the CDS intellectually or in the essential bargaining process between the two, and the line between the civilian and military operations blurred even further. Some deputies, notably Robert Fowler, who held power for the bleak years from 1989 to 1995, involved themselves directly in operational matters and even went into the field to hear the reports of "their" generals.

In these trying times for the Canadian Forces, the blame tended to fall—wrongly—on Paul Hellyer. It was a bit like the old Prairie farmer, whose response to every catastrophe in the 1900s, from hail to low wheat prices, was to blame "the goddamn CPR." Even so, perhaps the time had come to look at what Hellyer had wrought.

When Joe Clark won the 1979 election, his Defence Minister, Allan McKinnon, a retired army major, announced a review of unification. After a decade, however, such an investigation was akin to unscrambling eggs, and the military advice was to not proceed. "Why should we reopen that can of worms?" they inquired. But the Minister proceeded, and his committee, led by retired businessman George Fyffe, found to its surprise that the environments were not completely unhappy. Morale was poor, but unification was not the only, or even the most important, reason. Rather, the military was most frustrated by low budgets in an era of soaring inflation.

The Fyffe Committee's recommendation was to retain a unified force but to give the environments back their distinctive uniforms and to cede their chiefs more clout at headquarters in Ottawa. Fyffe said that the heads of the three services had to be in Ottawa, with a Chiefs of Staff organization that could reduce the "civilianization" of the Canadian Forces. They needed "a voice at the table" to put the "focus back on operations."

The hapless Clark government was out of power by the time the committee delivered its report, and the restored Trudeau administration refused to allow distinctive uniforms. It was difficult to justify spending from $36 to $100 million on new uniforms when soldiers lacked weapons, naval ships verged on foundering, and aircraft could not fly because of shortages of spare parts. Yet the distinctive uniforms issue returned when Brian Mulroney's Progressive Conservative government took power in 1984. Defence Minister Robert Coates authorized the "Coates of many colours" in his brief tenure of office. These uniforms ought not to have made a huge difference, except that parades took on a varied look, with different-suited men and women all marching, or shambling, along together. Unfortunately, the Canadian Forces seemed to have decided that crisp drill and a smart appearance were unnecessary aspects of military life. It all verged on the absurd.

In June 1994 I was at Green Park in London with CBC-TV for the dedication of a memorial to the million Canadian servicemen and women who had served in Britain in the two world wars. A guard from the Canadian Forces took part, its composition carefully balanced to reflect the gender-neutral and multicultural organization it was. Unfortunately, no one had taught the Canadians how to do simple foot-and-rifle drill well, and the British Guardsmen on parade were the only ones who looked like soldiers. I was not alone in feeling embarrassed for the Canadian contingent. Appearances do matter.

As unification gradually weakened in the Canadian Forces, the environments assumed more and more of the old service prerogatives. The Chief of the Defence Staff and his senior commanders at National Defence Headquarters had begun losing their control over the Canadian Forces after the 1972 amalgamation of headquarters, a process accelerated by the 1980 decision to give the environmental commanders more clout. The NDHQ staff's ability to plan effectively, to operate in the internecine Ottawa bureaucracy, similarly came into doubt. The Chiefs of the Land Staff, Air Staff, and Maritime Staff returned to Ottawa in the 1990s and began to acquire almost all the powers and perquisites their predecessors had had before unification became the law in 1968. Committees at NDHQ started to multiply, and the triplication of functions began to creep back. The navy effectively ran its own promotion system, as did army regiments, all but bypassing the unified promotion system The army created its own staff college to hand down special-to-service knowledge not taught by the Canadian Forces Command and Staff College in north Toronto. Environmental commanders began to claim that trades specialists were not properly prepared by Canadian Forces engineering courses, for example, and insisted that the air force (or the navy or the army) run its own programs, even though 80 percent of the course content was common to all three services.

Most important, the fighting over budgets and the disputes about strategic thinking (or the lack of it) were as sharp as they had ever been. The Chief of the Land Staff in late June 2003 argued it was "unlikely" that the Canadian Forces "will be called upon to fight in 'blue skies or blue waters'" and, therefore, it made sense to put all the available money into army needs. The other chiefs' reactions were predictably apoplectic, and confrontation resumed at NDHQ.

In the early years of the twenty-first century, thirty-five

years after the unification of the services, some intelligent senior officers were beginning to argue that it was time to unify the Canadian Forces once more. In a tiny military with limited funds, divisive strategic concepts and a wasteful organization are simply intolerable. Where is Paul Hellyer now that we really need him?

CHAPTER 4

Malign Neglect:
Pierre Trudeau and
the Politics of Indifference

W HO killed the Canadian military? Pierre Trudeau, the most intelligent Prime Minister of the modern era. Trudeau had not the slightest interest in or appreciation of the Canadian Forces. His indifference and his anti-military attitudes typified the views of most *Canadiens* and a great many Canadians.

Born in Montreal in 1919, the son of an entrepeneur who made a fortune with a chain of gas stations, Pierre Trudeau was twenty when the Second World War broke out, a student at the Collège Jean-de-Brébeuf. He went on to the Université de Montréal, where he was made to join the Canadian Officers Training Corps, an obligation he treated as a joke, and then to serve in a reserve battalion of the Fusiliers Mont-Royal, another wartime lark. "I was bored by the present," he recalled. Luckily for him, he was not ordered to go on active service, and he viewed the war from the perspective of a Quebec *nationaliste*. In this view, Canada was not threatened; rather, it was a British war, a war of imperialisms of no concern to Canada. If English Canada pined to help England, then let it, so long as French Canadians were not forced to participate. Those who wished to could volunteer, just as others could work in war factories. But Québécois should not be made to do anything against their will for the national war effort. Trudeau and other nationalist youth who gathered around André Laurendeau, the editor of *L'action nationale*, were not the only ones to hold such opinions; so did the Catholic Church and the Quebec opposition led by Maurice Duplessis.

During the conscription plebiscite campaign in early 1942, when Laurendeau led the opposition to the federal government, Trudeau appears not to have spoken for the *non* at public meetings, though he almost certainly voted no. He did, however, make speeches in a federal by-election in Outremont in late 1942 for Jean Drapeau, the candidate of the anti-conscriptionist and pro-Vichy Bloc Populaire Canadien, which grew out of the *non* campaign. His *nationaliste* and anti-war views did not begin to change until he went to Harvard University in 1944, his freshly minted law degree in hand. To his surprise, he discovered there were few men in his classes, for most fit males had joined the United States armed forces. The war was important in Boston, and everyone took it seriously, as a matter of life and death for democracy and freedom. It was not a British imperialist war, but a fight for the survival of the democracies and the defeat of Nazism, Fascism, and Japanese militarism. Highly intelligent as he was, Trudeau recalled that his time at Harvard confirmed his beliefs "about individual freedom." He had lived in a closed society with few dissentient voices, and he had completely missed the significance of the Second World War for global freedom. In this, he was typical of the intellectual, nationalist youth of French Canada—and their elders.

Trudeau's term at Harvard and his travels to Europe immediately after the war began to open his eyes. When he returned to Montreal in 1949, he was ready to oppose the conformist attitudes and closed minds of Duplessis's Quebec. But for a long time he was almost alone, a critic who was not honoured in his own society. Quebec was reactionary and cloistered, and it remained so for another decade. In the context of this book, however, Trudeau was not the odd man out. He and Quebec remained united in a profound antimilitary attitude that needs to be explored before we look at Trudeau's policies in office.

The history dates back at least to the Conquest in 1759, which drove France from North America and left the *habitants* to the mercies of the British. The French Canadians had flirted with the invading Americans in 1775 and, with some notable exceptions aside, had been largely indifferent to the War of 1812. The new Dominion of Canada had begun the process of creating national military institutions, but, as a British colony, conscious of the need to keep the Old Country involved in Canada's defence, its military looked and acted British and almost always spoke English. When the rebellion of 1885 roiled the political waters, Quebec militia units joined in suppressing the Métis, but when the French-speaking Louis Riel was executed on a gibbet in Regina, Quebec believed it had been betrayed. The South African War fifteen years later did nothing to change that sense. The dominion government was forced by English-speaking Cabinet ministers and the media to send troops to help Britain suppress the Boers, a people who were, in French Canada's eyes, similar to the *Canadiens*. That the government was led by Sir Wilfrid Laurier, the country's first French-speaking Prime Minister, made the Quebec resentment even greater.

The Great War in 1914 compounded all the problems and made them permanent. It mattered little that France and Britain were allied or that France faced imminent invasion from Germany; the war was a British war as far as Quebec was concerned. Canada, a colony of London, was obliged to participate, but it did not take long before English-speaking citizens began to count the numbers of volunteers by their linguistic origin. In the first contingent of 31,300, dispatched overseas in October 1914, only 1,245 officers and men were French-speaking. Although some two-thirds of the contingent was born in Britain, English-speaking Canada concluded that Quebec had failed the test of loyalty to crown and empire.

There were reasons for this indifference, most of them good. The Canadian soldiers drilled, trained, and fought in English, and that language restriction kept thousands of unilingual French-speakers out of the forces either from indignation or from fear they would suffer discrimination. Single men were preferred as soldiers, moreover, but Quebeckers tended to marry earlier and have more children than their compatriots. Their level of health was generally poorer and, as in all agrarian provinces, farmers were slower to join up than urban dwellers. At root was the fact that francophones were attached to Canada and had few ties to Europe; they had, after all, been here for 300 years, far longer than the English-speakers. The rush to the colours among the British-born was proof that the shorter the time in Canada, the greater the interest in volunteering to serve the Old Country.

In wartime, unfortunately, few were willing to be rational. English Canadians persisted in their sneers at Quebec, while French Canadians argued that the real threat to franco- phones was in the assimilationist attitudes practised in the schools of Ontario and in Anglo racism. Very simply, in English Canada there was pressure to join up; in Quebec, to stay out. And countless thousands in *la belle province* did stay out. Those who enlisted tended to be adventurers, the jobless, or members of the elite—the Talbot Papineaus, Georges Vaniers, and Thomas Tremblays—who determined to do their bit as Quebeckers and become good, brave soldiers. A great many did. Quebec has always had a strong tradition of military service, but this small stream of volunteers tended to be washed away by the great river of opposition to participation.

We lack hard data on the total number of French-speaking enlistees in the First World War, but no one who has studied the question suggests there were even 50,000, a number that includes conscripts called up in the last year of the war and francophones from outside Quebec. In all, this number amounted at most to one in twelve or thirteen of the total in the Canadian Expeditionary Force, at a time when French Canadians made up more than a third of the Canadian population. At the same time, it wasn't until the end of the Great War that native-born Canadians outnumbered the British-born in the Canadian Expeditionary Force, an indication that English-speaking voluntarism was considerably less than myth remembers it. Still, it is inescapably true that Québécois did not serve in the war in anything like proportionate numbers.

Nonetheless, Quebec felt aggrieved, and conscription, the involuntary enlistment of men for military service, put the seal on the province's resentment. Sir Robert Borden's

102

government hesitantly introduced compulsory service in May 1917, effected it after the election of December, and faced riots and widespread evasion when it tried to enforce it in 1918. Riots in Quebec City were put down by a Toronto unit, an unfortunate choice. It was one thing for Québécois who wished to join up to fight in an Anglo war; it was another matter entirely for Ottawa politicians to force francophones to fight in "their" war. Conscription obliged men to risk and perhaps give their lives, and that was the most serious use of state power imaginable. In Quebec, 115,000 of the 117,000 men called for service, or 98.3 percent, sought an exemption, a terrifying demonstration of the unanimity of opinion. What English-Canadian critics then and since forget is that, in Ontario, 118,000 of the 125,000 called, or 94.4 percent, sought exemption. For French or English conscripts alike, the front was not the place to be.

Sir Robert Borden had wanted conscription to produce 100,000 men for the front and, had the war continued past November 11, 1918, his measure would have done so. But if conscription was intended to force French Canadians to fight, the results were less clear. Government records prepared a decade after the war found that there were 64,745 English-speaking conscripts and 27,557 French-speaking. The exemption tribunals in Quebec, or so a judge who served on the national appeal tribunal said, "gave exemptions automatically to French-Canadians. . . . But they applied conscription against the English-speaking minority in Quebec with a rigor unparalleled."

The Canadian Corps, historians have said repeatedly, was the embodiment of Canadian nationalism. But that's not true—the Corps was English-Canadian nationalism incarnate, and, at the front, there was only a single battalion of Québécois, the gallant 22ᵉ Bataillon. The war was a tragedy for all nations, but for Canada the most enduring result was an even deeper racial and linguistic divide.

By 1939 little had changed to knit the Canadian fabric together again. Mackenzie King, the Prime Minister for most of the interwar years, had made Canada's foreign policy into the isolationist catch phrase used by Senator Raoul Dandurand in an address to the Assembly of the League of Nations in October 1924: "We live in a fire-proof house far from inflammable materials." King added his own shorthand phrase of avoidance: "Parliament will decide." Activist F.R. Scott, one of Canada's leading poets and a stalwart in the social democratic Cooperative Commonwealth Federation, observed in 1938 that Canada's foreign policy was "a policy of drift," moving wherever circumstances took it. Events determined policy, not rational thought, he said, because the government's object was to keep international quarrels away for fear they might, once more, divide French and English Canada. This conscious and deliberate absence of policy meant that Canada offered no advance commitments on any matter of foreign or defence policy, a tactic that generally kept Quebec happily within the Liberal fold. King also ignored domestic military spending, a policy that, in the 1920s and the Depression years, had few critics anywhere in Canada and certainly none in Quebec. It is probably fair to say that French Canada's concerns drove interwar Canadian foreign and defence policy, but in truth there was little public interest in the subjects anywhere. When war came again in September 1939, Mackenzie King moved, as he had no doubt always intended, to support Britain.

This time, however, Canada went to war by the decision of its own Parliament, not as a colony. The King government had learned one lesson of the Great War and, six months before the war began, promised there would be no conscription for overseas service. Quebec grudgingly accepted participation on those terms and on the implicit understanding that the war, for Canada, was one of limited liability. The nation, in other words, was not a great power, its territory was not directly threatened, and the most important issue was not victory but the preservation of national unity.

Meanwhile, the 22ᵉ Bataillon had become the Royal 22ᵉ Régiment, a Permanent Force infantry regiment that would add notably to its Great War laurels in Sicily, Italy, and Northwest Europe. Eventually there were three additional battalions of French-speaking infantry and some artillery units overseas, as well as thousands of sailors and aircrew.

105

But the armed forces still drilled, trained, and fought in English. There were only a handful of French-speaking senior army officers and almost none in the Royal Canadian Navy or the Royal Canadian Air Force, despite Ottawa's efforts to find good men and promote them as the war went on. Some of Canada's best fighting leaders—Jean-Victor Allard, Paul Bernatchez, and "Mad Jimmy" Dextraze, to cite only three superb examples—rose through the ranks because of their skill and courage to command battalions and brigades with distinction. English Canadians nonetheless gave full vent once again to their resentment at what they perceived as their Quebec countrymen's reluctance to fight.

Part of the difficulty was attitude. In December 1941 the Defence Minister, Colonel J.L. Ralston, explained his views to his Deputy Minister (who promptly passed them on to a journalist friend): "The army would not have masses of Quebeckers under any conditions; they would not be able to do anything with them. There is only limited room in our army for these men. They can't speak English. We have no French-Canadian officers to handle them. Their fighting ability is questionable, etc. etc." This kind of bigotry was the mirror image of the francophone attitude that the war was not theirs to fight. Which came first—the Anglo bigotry or the Quebec unconcern? Once again the Canadian penchant for putting difficult questions aside to resolve later, years

106

after the Great War, had proved to be a mistake of historic proportions.

Conscription for home defence, imposed after the fall of France in 1940, was generally accepted in Quebec. Québécois had always claimed they were ready to defend Canada and, in the summer of 1940 after Dunkirk, the possibility of threat to the homeland seemed real enough. Nonetheless, André Laurendeau and friends feared that home defence was merely the first bite at the cherry of compulsory service, a view confirmed for them in 1942 when Ottawa asked Canadians in a plebiscite to release the government from its pre-war promise of no overseas conscription. The plebiscite results demonstrated yet again the two solitudes in Canada. Quebec voted 72.9 percent *non*, a percentage reduced by the anglophone vote in Montreal and the Eastern Townships. In Ontario 82.3 percent voted yes; in Alberta, 70.4 percent; and in New Brunswick, 69.1. Everywhere in Canada, francophones and ethnic voters heavily voted no. Still, Mackenzie King had the overall result he wanted, and he put legislation through Parliament to permit conscription for overseas service.

King's policies had been determined by his desire and need to keep Quebec on side. The Liberals controlled Quebec, and Quebec to a large extent controlled the Liberals, at least insofar as manpower questions were concerned. Opinion polls left no doubt that English Canada wanted conscription as much as Quebec did not, and King had manoeuvred from 1939 to late 1944 to avoid it. He almost succeeded, but was forced into it by the threat of Cabinet revolt and the pressing needs of the front.

It was not until November 1944, faced with a shortage of infantry at the fronts, that Ottawa ordered overseas 16,000 of the 60,000 Zombies, as the home defence conscripts were derisively labelled. The reaction in French Canada to this half-measure was sharp, and Quebec and the rest of Canada at once came to believe that all the reluctant soldiers were French. In fact, the home defence soldiers were only 37-percent French-speaking. Nonetheless, very few francophones supported sending the conscripts overseas, and for a large number of Québécois, the federal Liberals under Mackenzie King, just like the Conservatives under Sir Robert Borden in the Great War, had betrayed Quebec. No government dominated by English-speakers could ever be trusted to respect French Canada's desire to turn its back on the world and its problems.

As in 1914–18, the pressures in English Canada were to enlist in the great crusade for democracy. The attitude in Quebec, which Pierre Trudeau clearly shared, was to avoid joining up in another Anglo war. Still, an estimated 150,000 francophone volunteers and conscripts served, just under 15 percent of the 1.1 million Canadian men and women who put on the uniform. This number was well below French Canada's proportionate share of the population, but, compared with the First World War, the Quebec military effort was three times as large. This was a huge triumph, a tribute to government efforts to bring the population along slowly and carefully, to educate the people about the stakes at risk. It was also a tribute to those men and women from Quebec who recognized there were great issues at stake, issues that would determine the fate of freedom and the democracies. Most Quebeckers, however, including Trudeau, did not join up.

Quebec's wariness about war continued into the next decade. Louis St. Laurent, Canada's second French-speaking Prime Minister, was hugely popular in his home province and, alone among post-war Canadian leaders, took risks in Quebec in campaigning for his government's foreign and defence policy. His Cabinet was even ready to impose conscription if war with the Soviet Union erupted, as many feared it might. The cards for the necessary national registration were printed and stored, ready for issue. When a well-informed Liberal journalist privately asked Defence Minister Brooke Claxton how such a measure would be received in French Canada, the answer was unequivocal: "With this Prime Minister we can do anything in Quebec." Others believed this too. Blair Fraser wrote in *Maclean's* that "Quebec is not so firmly and deeply anti-war as it used to be." Yet St. Laurent won at best a grudging acquiescence

from French Canada both for his government's decision in
1949 to take Canada into NATO and for its participation in
Korea. At the beginning of the 1950s, to meet Canada's
NATO obligations, he dispatched a brigade group and an air
division for service in France and in Germany. Then, when
the Korean War began in mid-1950 on the opposite side of
the world, Canada, pressed by the United States to contribute, raised a brigade group for service in the first United
Nations "police action."

The armed forces were still overwhelmingly English-
speaking, however, the training manuals and orders were still
issued in English only, and opinion polls in Quebec showed a
massive lack of interest in the Korean War, the Cold War, and
the military. One survey found 83 percent of French
Canadians opposed to conscription for Korea, as close to
unanimity as polls ever get. Another showed only 21 percent
in favour of sending any troops to Korea, and 62 percent
opposed. Asked about dispatching troops to Europe, French
Canadians again expressed their opposition, 52 percent
against and 37 percent in support. St. Laurent's courage in
acting in the face of such polls deserves note. The key point is
that St. Laurent's power in Quebec was not threatened by his
foreign and defence policies. Presumably he delivered
enough in other areas to keep Quebeckers on side.

Still, there were other signs of French-Canadian indifference to foreign commitments. The Royal 22^e had trouble

finding recruits and junior officers to fill out its ranks throughout the Korean War, an indication that the conflict, not very popular anywhere in Canada, was even less so in Quebec. "There were just not enough French-speaking recruits coming forward," the official historian of the Army in Korea noted, "to enable [Royal 22^e] battalions to be brought up to strength and still retain their French-Canadian character." Data subsequently collected demonstrated that, in December 1950, only 12.3 percent of the Canadian Army was French-speaking, and representation in technical corps was even lower. Yet the army was the most French of the services. In the Royal Canadian Navy, only 2 percent of officers and 11 percent of ratings were francophones; in the Royal Canadian Air Force, 4 percent of officers and 16 percent of the men were French-speaking. Quebec went along grudgingly with St. Laurent, but it was fortunate he was not tested by the demands of a major war.

Was the root cause of Quebec's lack of interest the unilingual nature of the Canadian armed services? Francophones had been claiming so for years, but no one had done much to meet the problem. In 1952 the Collège militaire royal de St-Jean (CMR) opened its doors in Quebec as a military college designed to attract French-speaking cadets to be trained as junior officers for the army, navy, and air force. CMR was a bilingual institution, with anglophone and francophone cadets studying in their own language but doing everything else on a two-week rotation in both French and English. I was a CMR cadet from 1956 to 1959, and when I went to the Royal Military College in Kingston for the last two years of my course I was (briefly!) functionally bilingual; so were most other cadets, whether French- or English-speaking. For the Canadian military, CMR led the way in reflecting the nation's bicultural reality.

But it was only a start. Not until the Royal Commission on Bilingualism and Biculturalism in 1963 did Canada admit it had a linguistic and cultural problem threatening its survival—and the armed forces were part of that problem. Data collected in 1966 showed that 73 percent of Canadian Forces officers were of British origin and only 12.5 percent francophone; for enlisted ranks, the percentages were 63.0 and 20.3. Soon, pressure began to be exerted to right the balance, not least by the first francophone Chief of the Defence Staff, General Jean-Victor Allard. For years he had pushed for bilingualism and called for the creation of French-speaking units, but had made little headway. Now he was in a position to do something. After Paul Hellyer left the Defence Department in 1967, Allard had Léo Cadieux, another francophone, as Minister. Working together, and spurred on by the pending passage of the *Official Languages Act* (enacted in 1969), they transformed the military. The first French-speaking units were created: a brigade in Valcartier,

Quebec, 5e Groupement de Combat; a CF-5 squadron, No. 433, in Bagotville, Quebec; and a destroyer, NCSM *Ottawa*. "Now, we're going to have a 22^e of the sea and a 22^e of the air," Cadieux said. The training system was adapted to prepare francophones for service in their own language, including some of the trades training. Orders and manuals were translated, and soon virtually everything was *aussi disponible en français*. It was a huge change, as was Allard's insistence that francophones had to be present everywhere in the services and in all ranks, from private to general, in appropriate percentages. By the mid-1970s the Canadian Forces was to be 28-percent francophone—and it was.

In the eyes of some in Ottawa (and perhaps in Quebec City), what Cadieux and Allard were doing was unknowingly creating the armed forces of the *indépendantiste* Quebec Republic. With the revolutionary Front de libération du Québec (FLQ) active, with separatism making converts every day, with the charismatic René Lévesque leading a new party and calling for Quebec to leave Canada, did it make sense to have unilingual French-Canadian units concentrated in Quebec? Michael Pitfield, in the Privy Council Office, called it "one of the most potentially dangerous decisions the Federal government could ever take," one that could "irrevocably lay the groundwork for an exceedingly dangerous situation." Marc Lalonde, in the Prime Minister's Office, agreed: "We have to think here of the problems that such a concentration would cause in the case of a very serious political upheaval in the Province of Quebec."

When the October Crisis erupted in the autumn of 1970 and Trudeau's government imposed the *War Measures Act*, troops were sent in large numbers onto the streets of Montreal and other cities in Quebec. Yet the difficulties anticipated by Pitfield and Lalonde did not emerge. Canadian soldiers, francophone and anglophone alike, did their duty in exemplary fashion, and anyone with doubts about francophone soldiers' loyalty had those concerns dispelled.

The October Crisis, however, did nothing to make the bilingualism of the military any easier to achieve, and the resentment was fierce among anglophones who watched bitterly as French-speaking officers and non-commissioned officers progressed rapidly. Inevitably quotas led to some duds rising to high rank, their linguistic skills seemingly their only qualifications. Good francophone officers worried that their promotions were based not on merit but on linguistic skill. Was it "part of the charade"? one general remembered hearing from a few of his staff. Some units were disbanded so that French Language Units could be created (the Canadian Guards, the Black Watch, and other "British-sounding" and "British-appearing" units disappeared), and servicemen whose brain could not grasp the other language, no matter how many language classes they attended, slowly began to recognize that their careers had been blighted. To some, bilingualism meant that, like parentheses, "we had to have two of everything"—two languages, two speeches at a meeting, two manuals, perhaps even two ways of doing things. It was a sea change, if a wholly necessary one.

By 1997, the government decreed, functional bilingualism would be a requirement for promotion to the rank of lieutenant-colonel or higher. The process of transformation had been a success, and francophones could no longer justly complain that the Canadian Forces was unwelcoming. Whether these changes have altered Quebec's historic attitudes to military service remains unknown.

Other processes were simultaneously under way as the bilingualization of the armed forces proceeded apace. The military had been unified, and many old and honoured traditions had been discarded. Budgets were frozen or slashed, equipment grew obsolescent, missions altered in scope and duration, and anti-Americanism continued to be a powerful sentiment even as the Canadian Forces' links with the superpower's military grew stronger. Most important, Pierre Trudeau was in power as Prime Minister from 1968 to 1984, with only a few months out in opposition in 1979–80.

Trudeau had a low opinion of the military, which he believed to be populated by robots trained to kill. He asked

Bill Lee, the Liberal Party's campaign tour organizer in the 1968 election and a former RCAF wing commander, "Why would a guy as smart as you waste his time in the military?" The generals and their soldiers were brutes and dolts, frittering away their time and the government's money. The military was simply too expensive to maintain, unnecessary for a nation as safe from attack—in his eyes—as Canada. Moreover, as Trudeau came to power, the United States found itself trapped in a swamp of its own making in Vietnam. The US Army had already begun to fall apart under the strain of a guerrilla war, the "fragging" of unpopular officers killed by their own soldiers, and an era of massive dissent. Why should Canada even bother with an army in such a climate?

Trudeau's views were evident from the first days after he came to power. The Prime Minister set out to reassess Canada's policy in the world, and he focused his gaze on the country's NATO contribution. In a talk to the Alberta Liberal Association in April 1969, an audience expectantly awaiting word on the government's oil policy, Trudeau instead outlined the rationale for the alterations he was about to make to Canada's defence and foreign policies. "In the situation we had reached," he said, "NATO had in reality determined all of our defence policy. . . . And our defence policy had determined all of our foreign policy." In these circumstances, he continued, "we had no foreign policy of any importance except that which flowed from NATO. And this is a false perspective . . . to have a military alliance determine your foreign policy. It should be your foreign policy which determines your military policy."

To reach his assessment, Trudeau had conducted a series of "seminars" with his Cabinet where he made the case—perhaps as an academic exercise—for a complete withdrawal of the brigade group and the air division of CF-104s from Europe. His Defence and External Affairs Ministers were horrified and talked of resignation, but by April 1969 Trudeau had graciously conceded that perhaps 3,500 men could remain in NATO. The brigade group, once one of the most effective units in NATO, according to historian Lieutenant-Colonel Jack English, had at a stroke been "reduced to one of the least effective." The strength Trudeau agreed to retain in NATO eventually rose to 5,000, but the air force's nuclear role in Europe was to be abandoned by 1972. (In Canada, fighters under NORAD continued to be armed with nuclear weapons for another decade.) At the same time, the defence budget was frozen at $1.8 billion (or roughly $7 billion in 1992–93 dollars), and the percentage of the federal budget devoted to defence catapulted downward from 18 percent in 1967–68 to 13 percent four years later. The percentage of gross domestic product spent on the military similarly declined from 2.5 to 2 percent. The strength of the Canadian Forces fell between 1968 and 1974 by 17,000 all ranks to around 80,000. Not even the October 1970 FLQ Crisis changed Trudeau's mind. The military performed extraordinarily well in Quebec, but efficient police, or so the Prime Minister seemed to think, could have done the job just as well.

Trudeau's first Defence Minister, Léo Cadieux, strongly supported the idea that Canada should meet its commitments to its allies, so it would be unjust to say that Trudeau's attitude to the Canadian military and its NATO commitments was typically French Canadian. Yet in some ways it was—particularly the views of the young Trudeau of Second World War days. The contrarian Trudeau may have left behind the anti-war and pro-Vichy *nationalistes* who had been his friends then, but his attitudes to the world in 1968 were still as isolationist and anti-military at root as they had been a quarter-century before. The world had changed, but in his fundamental attitudes to it, Trudeau remained fixed in the concrete straitjacket of his youth.

He had travelled widely all his life and studied abroad. He had seen Europe in the aftermath of Nazism and war, but his journeys had served only to reinforce his iconoclasm. He perhaps understood the United States less well than any of his prime ministerial predecessors, and he might fairly be called anti-American. His government made a specialty of "pissing" on the American rug, to use Lyndon Johnson's pungent phrase. Whatever his virtues, Trudeau knew little of the

United States and its global responsibilities. He proved indifferent enough to the Cold War to slash Canada's 10,000-man commitment to NATO in half and to cut the strength of the armed forces. His talk of "equivalence," as if the USSR and the United States were equivalent threats to Canada and the world, was awesomely stupid in its pandering to anti-American Canadians and it rightly upset Presidents Richard Nixon and Ronald Reagan. His "peace initiative" in 1983–84 at the end of his time in power infuriated the Americans, then deeply embroiled in disputes with Leonid Brezhnev's Moscow.

Trudeau had the misfortune to coincide with Nixon and Reagan, Gerald Ford and Jimmy Carter, four of the least inspiring American Presidents of modern times. Compared with Brezhnez and the rest of the lacklustre recycled Stalinists who made up the Politburo, however, the Americans should have seemed giants. Yet, if Trudeau had got his way, Canada would have been as neutral as he could make it in the Cold War, civil to both the USSR and the United States, but allied to neither. In this regard, he reflected the majority Quebec opinion of the 1970s and 1980s (and much of the extreme English-Canadian nationalist opinion too), one that paradoxically wanted as much free trade as it could get with the United States but as little to do with it in other matters as possible. When Trudeau left power, relations with the Reagan Administration were as bad as those

119

Jean Chrétien would have with the administration of George W. Bush almost two decades later. The Americans saw Trudeau as "a leftist high on pot"—the comment of a Reagan Administration official. Silly as that was, it reflected the US disdain for a Canadian leader who had essentially missed the point on the great issues of the day.

If Trudeau had got his way, Canada would also have had armed forces that stayed home to preserve domestic tranquility and order. "Sovereignty" was the first defence buzzword of Trudeau's time, and after the October Crisis, "internal security" was the next. As officers recalled, if you could say that helicopters could do sovereignty patrols and, with a few lights attached, be useful for internal security, "you might get the government to buy them. If not . . ." There were good reasons for this comment. Trudeau's determination to keep Quebec in Canada at a time when the FLQ terrorists had their supporters throughout francophone society demanded that he be prepared to protect the state against those who would destroy it. But there were threats from outside Canada too, and Trudeau seemed all but blind to them. He cut the country's NATO contribution a short time after the USSR and its Warsaw Pact allies invaded Czechoslovakia and crushed the "Prague Spring" in 1968. He was cool to any build-up of NATO's missile strength, no matter what the Soviets did—and they were doing plenty. He did agree to the purchase of CF-18 fighters for the air force, thanks to a skilful campaign by his Defence Minister Barney Danson and fine staff work from within the air force, and he accepted the construction of six frigates in Canada; in both purchases, the industrial offsets and jobs created in Quebec and the Maritimes were likely more important to the Prime Minister than the weapons systems. Trudeau also agreed to new tanks for the rump Canadian brigade in NATO because he thought a purchase of German Leopards might win him points with Chancellor Helmut Schmidt and help get Canada a good trade arrangement with the European Community.

During its long period in power, the Trudeau government began the "rust-out" of the Canadian Forces' equipment, as replacement of weapons systems was first delayed, then delayed again, and finally postponed. The gap between Canada's commitments, which Trudeau scarcely believed in, and the Canadian Forces' capabilities, which he thought unimportant, grew substantially. Defence specialist Rod Byers observed that by the early 1980s, "fiscal considerations had a more profound effect on Canada's military posture than did military-strategic requirements . . . defence issues were not a priority."

To Trudeau, the Canadian Forces was an alien nation of almost no importance. Money spent on the military was money wasted. Who, after all, had any intention of threatening Canada other than the FLQ? His attitudes turned into policy, and he ran down the forces' strength and allowed its equipment to slide towards obsolescence. What more was needed to preserve domestic order than an ill-armed constabulary and a Prime Minister with the will to use it on the streets of Montreal? By 1984 the Canadian Forces' strength was at 82,000, and all three services faced major equipment and personnel problems. The navy was in the worst shape. Only four of its twenty-three warships were less than twenty years old, a few verged on being unsafe to put to sea, and some navy electronics systems required vacuum tubes obtainable only in Eastern Europe.

The pressure to remedy the military's problems became so strong from Washington and NATO capitals that even Trudeau had to act. In the late 1970s NATO governments pledged to increase defence funding by 3 percent above inflation each year. Trudeau went along with this agreement and, indeed, lived up to the promise. But the deficiencies of two decades could not be remedied overnight.

Fundamentally, Trudeau was an isolationist on the main issues of foreign policy—the Cold War issues of the 1960s, 1970s, and 1980s.* He turned himself into a supporter of the Commonwealth and la Francophonie, enjoyed G-7 meetings, and talked a good line on Developing World aid

---

*Parenthetically, this was why no one outside the Parti Québécois backrooms believed René Lévesque when he claimed that an independent Quebec would stay in NORAD and NATO. It was a transparent effort to get US support, but Washington surely was not fooled.

questions. He was no traditional *nationaliste* isolationist, any more than Quebec in the 1970s was, but he again reflected and helped to reinforce the traditional francophone attitude that the world's troubles and wars could never really affect Quebec and Canada, safe behind the oceans.* What mattered to Québécois was their status, their place, in Canada and, secondarily, in North America. That Trudeau appeared to accept this view in a Cold War world suggested an utter naïveté that was curious in a man of powerful intellect. It was a reflection of his inconsistency, his dilettantism, his tendency to dabble only in the issues that interested him. What seems clear is that the central issues of foreign policy that divided the West and the Communist world did not greatly concern Trudeau— aside from his peace initiative of 1983–84. Perhaps he simply believed that Canada could have no real impact on them. Even if he doubled the defence budget and the size of the Canadian Forces, nothing would change.

Steadfast small allies are important. They inspire other small nations to do their part, and groups of allies can and

---

*Nothing seems to have changed in Quebec. An opinion poll for the Canadian Defence and Foreign Affairs Institute and the Dominion Institute (published September 6, 2003) found that Québécois oppose the rebuilding of the Canadian Forces, only 41 percent seeing a need to do so and almost one in three arguing that the United States will protect Canada "so we don't need to spend a lot." If they support any military role, it is peacekeeping (61 percent in favour versus 46 percent in the rest of the country).

do sway the decisions of their superpower leaders. On the whole, English-speaking Canadians, their traditions and attitudes shaped by a history of serving in imperial coalitions, appeared more ready to accept that allies who play their role can have some influence with the superpowers—certainly more than if they do nothing. Paul Martin Sr., Canada's Secretary of State for External Affairs in 1967 and a Franco-Ontarian who understood both his country and international affairs far better than Trudeau, remarked that many nations had "an appetite for power without teeth." During the Cold War, he noted, Canada "had developed both the appetite and the teeth for a new international role." Trudeau didn't even try to understand this point, and, during his long reign, the military teeth that gave some bite to Canada's place in the world rapidly began to decay. When he launched his quixotic peace initiative of 1983–84, he was met with a frosty reception from the Soviets, Americans, British, French, and Chinese as he travelled around the world, demonstrating that, by the time he left office, no one paid much attention to his toothless Canada. Ultimately, his approach was futile. Hailed as a friend of the Third World, Trudeau began the process of making Canada irrelevant in the important business of the First World. Over sixteen years in power, he succeeded in making the Canadian Forces as weak and irrelevant as he left Canadian foreign policy. Without a doubt, Pierre Trudeau killed the Canadian Forces.

CHAPTER 5

The False Dawn of Hope: The Mulroney Years

BRIAN Mulroney promised to restore Canada's relations with the United States and did so, though not everyone cheered his efforts. He also promised to rebuild the Canadian Forces, to give the army, navy, and air force the personnel, the budgets, and the tools to do their jobs. Just as Mulroney pledged to fix the country's budget deficit but signally failed to do so, so he raised the military's hopes repeatedly but failed to deliver. Meanwhile, Mulroney's government made the Canadian Forces a bastion of political correctness but, by accepting every peacekeeping role despite the forces' emaciated condition, he plunged it into the morass of Somalia. Who killed the Canadian military? Brian Mulroney did.

When he was in opposition, Brian Mulroney played on the weakness of the Canadian Forces. If the Progressive Conservatives won the coming election, his party spokesmen said, Canada's long dark night of military embarrassment would come to an end. Canada and the United States were neighbours and friends, allies in the Cold War against the

Soviet Union. There would be no more Trudeauesque flirtations with neutrality, no more senseless pulling at the eagle's tail feathers. The strength of the Canadian Forces, wasted away to 82,000 under two decades of Grit rule, would be increased to 92,000, and defence spending would rise by 4 percent a year. During the 1984 election campaign, Mulroney himself upped the ante, pledging a 6-percent annual budget increase and an immediate infusion of $190 million to recruit 2,200 men and women in one year, provide distinctive service uniforms, and begin to meet the shortfall in capital spending. All this sounded good to the Canadian Forces—a government that would look out for its interests, and Canada's.

The troubles to come were apparent as soon as Mulroney took over. The Tories confirmed what they already knew: the nation's fiscal situation was serious, the budget deficits having soared under a profligate Liberal government. Many promises made in opposition and in the election campaign would have to remain unmet or be delayed.

The first hint of unpleasantness for the Canadian Forces came when the new Prime Minister appointed his Minister of National Defence. Mulroney's choice was Robert Coates, a lacklustre Nova Scotia MP whose only claim to preferment was his opposition to the previous Conservative leader, Joe Clark, and his political positions, all firmly on the party's right wing. Coates came to power suspicious of his new department's bureaucracy and, within weeks, he and his personal office staff were fighting with civilian and military officials at the Department of National Defence. Coates wanted the new uniforms, even though the Chief of the Defence Staff made clear that the capital equipment needs of the Canadian Forces were far more important.

Coates made some of the right noises on equipment and personnel. He promised a "green paper" on defence for early in 1985 and pledged to increase the existing six-frigate building program to twelve ships, the additional cost being $4.5 billion. (The twelve-ship program would end up costing a total of $10 billion, including some funds for the upgrading of Saint John's shipbuilding yards.) He said he would raise the strength of Canadian troops in NATO and pointed out that some $10 billion was needed to rectify the equipment shortfalls the government had inherited from the Liberals. Coates, however, soon learned all about budget deficits, and in October 1984 he opined that major defence spending had to wait until "there is some kind of financial read of just how desperate the financial situation is at home."

Desperate indeed. In November 1984 Finance Minister Michael Wilson reduced defence spending to $9.37 billion (or $11.5 billion in 1992–93 dollars), a drop of $154 million from the budget presented just months before by Trudeau's Minister of Finance, Marc Lalonde. Canada was not going to meet its NATO pledge to increase defence spending by

129

3 percent a year above inflation, the first time it had failed to do so since 1979. Mulroney's campaign promise of an immediate infusion of $190 million also disappeared, compounding the shock to the Defence Department. Soon Coates too disappeared, caught in a sex scandal when the press revealed, during his visit to the Canadian NATO base at Lahr, Germany, that he had paid a late-night visit to Tiffany's, a sleazy strip club that was home to prostitutes working out of its backrooms.

I remember interviewing an army Lieutenant-General at National Defence Headquarters in connection with a book I was writing on the Mulroney government. It was just before Coates's self-immolation. "Was the Mulroney government going to be better for the CF?" I asked. "It'd better be," came the General's answer, "because it's the last chance for the military." The first months of the Tory government had not been good for the Canadian Forces.

There was soon a new Minister to deal with that last chance, as Erik Nielsen took the job. Nielsen was the Prime Minister's hatchet man, a dedicated party loyalist who held a powerful place in the inner circles of the Cabinet as Deputy Prime Minister. A decorated RCAF Bomber Command veteran of the Second World War, Nielsen quickly promised a defence White Paper to chart the way ahead for the Canadian Forces and announced an increase of 1,200 troops in the army's NATO brigade. He followed with the announcement of a $7-billion upgrade to North America's radar defences, with the United States paying 90 percent and Canada the remainder. It seemed almost too good to be true. Unfortunately, it was.

The budget of February 1986 made clear that no matter how powerful the Defence Minister might be, the Minister of Finance still held the whip hand. The generals had confidently expected that Mulroney's pledges of a 6-percent increase would be fulfilled at last, but DND learned it would get only 2.75 percent more in 1986–87 and 2.5 percent the following year. The whoosh of air as the balloon of expectations deflated could be heard all over Ottawa. Capital programs had to be deferred yet again, the White Paper was on hold, and, although NATO troop strength was increased by 970 men and the Canadian Forces received authority to increase overall strength by 1,752 (not the 10,000 Mulroney had promised), it was all terribly disappointing. Some of the generals now believed there was no future for the Canadian military. The last chance had collapsed.

But perhaps not. When Nielsen departed from National Defence in 1986, the young, ambitious Perrin Beatty arrived. Beatty was out to make his mark, and he slated preparation of the promised White Paper as his top priority. He delivered *Challenge and Commitment: A Defence Policy for Canada* the next year, and it was everything the Canadian Forces could have asked for. The White Paper's preface, written by the Minister, committed him and the government to giving the forces a "contemporary and manageable mandate" and "the resources necessary to do the job." "I agree fully with these priorities," Beatty wrote. This statement was remarkable, a level of ministerial commitment unheard of for more than thirty years.

There was more to come in the White Paper. The introduction took roundhouse swings at the country's powerful peace movement, declaring "neutrality would be hypocrisy. Our security would continue to depend on the deterrence provided [by allies], but we would have opted out of any contribution to and, equally significantly, any say in the management of that deterrent." Moreover, the paper noted, the hopes of détente that had prevailed through the 1970s and into the 1980s had been "exaggerated," and the USSR was and would remain a serious threat to North America and the world, a superpower that "continues to seek to translate military power into political gain." The Cold War went on, in other words. The paper took note of these facts and stated bluntly: "This review has confirmed that we are not able to meet [our] commitments fully and effectively. After decades of neglect, there is indeed a significant 'commitment-capability gap.'" Wholesale changes were required, most notably a "steady, predictable and honest funding program based on coherent and consistent political leadership." Beatty pledged a "rolling five-year funding plan

132

... within a fifteen-year planning framework," along with real growth in the budget of 2 percent a year above inflation for that fifteen-year planning period. He also stated the obvious. The forces' equipment was "in an advanced state of obsolescence," and if rust-out continued, policy was certain to be determined by that fact alone.

The Minister said the government would get the Canadian Forces the new equipment it needed, and he promised a four-fold increase in the country's reserve forces, mostly in the militia, along with new tanks for the NATO brigade and a commitment to increase it to a division in the event of a crisis. Beatty also pledged to raise the air force's NATO strength to an air division if the Cold War heated up and, in addition, to fly more sovereignty patrols over Canada and Canadian waters. Most strikingly, the government announced a three-ocean policy, for the first time putting the Arctic into the Canadian maritime equation. Beatty's plan called for a fleet of ten to twelve nuclear-powered submarines, capable of under-ice operation, of surveillance in the Arctic, and of playing a useful role in the Atlantic and the Pacific. Estimates of the cost were a minimum of $8 billion in then-current dollars.

133

The submarine proposal had been around for two years. In 1985 the US Coast Guard had dispatched the icebreaker *Polar Sea* through the Northwest Passage without asking Ottawa's permission. This voyage had caused a popular outcry, and Jean Chrétien, speaking for the Liberal opposition, shouted that "the Americans are using their friendship with Mulroney to take away a piece of Canada." The *Globe and Mail* jumped in too, charging that the Americans were demonstrating "contempt for a feckless friend. Is Canada indefinitely to allow a bully to kick ice in its face?" Soon after, the Department of External Affairs sent a secret memorandum to Cabinet urging that the government buy four nuclear submarines for sovereignty purposes. National Defence officials, their eyes firmly focused on Europe, however, continued to argue that money spent on defending the North was money wasted. Sovereignty in the Arctic was simply not a priority for the Canadian Forces when the money could be better employed in buying surface ships, aircraft, and armoured vehicles to take on the Russians.

But that was then. Now that Defence Minister Beatty wanted the nuclear submarines, the navy sensibly decided it wanted submarines too. For a time, many of the nationalist critics of defence spending were thrown off stride by the nuclear submarine plan, which they viewed as directed against the United States. Any policy that protected Canadian sovereignty from Washington's depredations was good policy, or so the nationalists believed. Nonetheless, most soon rallied against the submarines on the grounds that nuclear propulsion was unsafe and might damage the pristine Arctic. Pro-defence critics of the government had been equally startled by the submarine commitment and, although most of them thought the sovereignty issue was not serious from a military perspective (however much they recognized its political force),* they realistically came to believe that the nuclear-powered submarines would be useful in the event of war for their ability to fight Soviet submarines in the North Atlantic.

Beatty and the Progressive Conservative government had offered the Canadian Forces almost everything it wanted—more money, more equipment, more of everything, including the promise that the government "will implement this program vigorously." Promises were only promises, of course, but for the military these were good promises on which to build careers and make plans. It is a moot point whether the government would have lived up to them over a fifteen-year planning framework. No administration can commit its successors to anything, and circumstances always determine government actions.

As the circumstances changed, Beatty's political promises diminished into might-have-beens. The rise to power of Mikhail Gorbachev in the USSR, the speeding up of the processes of *glasnost* and *perestroika*, and the acceleration of unrest in the Soviet satellites of Eastern Europe all caused the "evil Empire" to unravel. On the verge of economic

---

*In the view of the influential British weekly *The Economist*, the submarine plan was an "Arctic antic," largely attributable to the "anti-American plasma that flows through many Canadian veins."

implosion, Moscow's hold on much of the globe dissolved, as did the USSR itself. The Cold War quickly disintegrated. The communist superpower had turned out to be a Third World country with a superpower military, as some Westerners had long claimed, and soon even that superpower military was in disarray. So rapid was the change in the global balance that, as early as 1989, the Department of National Defence in Ottawa stated: "No one seriously believes that the current Soviet leadership has any intention of attacking Western Europe or North America."

Almost as soon as it was issued, therefore, the 1987 White Paper was a relic of late–Cold War history. Its assumptions had failed the test of time, its forecasts proven utterly incorrect. The nuclear submarines, which really had been intended more for anti-submarine warfare purposes than for sovereignty, quickly fell off the government's table, sinking without a trace. If there truly was an American challenge to Canadian sovereignty in the Arctic, other means—political will, for one—would be necessary to oppose it. Indeed, all the promises in the Beatty paper disappeared as nations rushed to seize their "peace dividend" by cutting military budgets and deployments. Mulroney reduced the nation's commitment to NATO by 1,400 troops in 1991 and changed the air force's role in Germany from ground attack to air defence. The Conservative government's February 1992 budget stipulated that Canada's brigade and air group in NATO would be returned to Canada, and they were soon gone. All that remained of Canada's forty-two-year commitment of forces for NATO in Europe were a handful of staff officers in NATO commands, a few aircrew on airborne surveillance (AWACS) patrols, and a paper promise to provide troops in an emergency.

The Minister of National Defence from 1991 to 1993, while these decisions were taken, was Marcel Masse. A Quebec separatist by inclination, Masse had no hesitation in finding new ways to save money. He ordered supply depots in eastern Canada to consolidate their operations—in Quebec. By 1995, the time of the second Quebec referendum, Mulroney and Masse had departed, but, in the most populous portion of the country, the Canadian Forces was dependent on supplies drawn from a base that might have fallen into the hands of a Parti Québécois republic. Canada won the referendum by the barest of margins and nothing unpleasant occurred—except widespread rumours that at least one general officer had engaged in discussions with the Quebec government about becoming the generalissimo of the Quebec armed forces. Prime Minister Mulroney might have minded the stores rather better than he did.

The same criticism can be applied to CF strength. In 1989 it was 88,000, but fell below 80,000 by the end of the Tory government in 1993. Morale plummeted as the strength of the forces dropped. The expectations created by Mulroney's promises before the 1984 election had been dashed by the appointment of Robert Coates as Defence Minister and the first budget cuts. Hope had been revived by Erik Nielsen's appointment, but the budgets again disappointed the troops. Finally, Perrin Beatty's White Paper turned out to be chimerical. The roller-coaster ride of expectations had ended at ground level, leaving no one with much hope.

For servicemen, there was more despair to come. The collapse of the Soviet Union did not leave the world in peace. Iraq had invaded Kuwait in August 1990, and the United States mobilized a great coalition to drive Saddam Hussein's armies and secret police out of the oil fields that provided Kuwait's wealth. National Defence Headquarters had plans ready to send the brigade that, in late 1990, was still at its bases at Lahr, Germany, but the government refused to agree. The Canadian Leopard tanks were not up to the standard of those fielded by the United States, the United Kingdom, and France, the main coalition forces, not to mention lesser states such as Saudi Arabia. There was substantial opposition to the Gulf War in Canada—"no blood for oil," protesters chanted, forgetting that a large state had invaded a smaller one with utmost brutality—and the Prime Minister hung back.

In the end, and to his credit, Mulroney took Canada into the coalition—after a fashion. Canada sent CF-18 fighters hampered by tight rules of engagement; ships that had been armed, in part, with anti-aircraft guns hauled out of naval and military museums; and a company of soldiers for airfield defence. It was a humiliating display of impotence, the culmination of thirty years of military neglect by governments, and the Canadian Forces watched from a distance as the Iraqi military was quickly destroyed by a coordinated coalition air and ground assault. After years of Liberal and Conservative cutbacks, Canada's military, aside from the navy, could do very little. The nation had already cashed in its peace dividend in the 1970s and 1980s, and the Canadian Forces were in a poor state. The commitment-capability gap Mulroney's government had declared real in the 1987 White Paper had grown even greater.

Many additional problems troubled the military. Still trying to cope with the stresses caused by the Tories' half-unravelling of unification and the impact of bilingualism, the Canadian Forces now had to respond to the Canadian Charter of Rights and Freedoms, which had come into force in 1982. The Charter obliged the services to deal with women better than they had in the past.

Women had served in the military since 1885, when the first nurses accompanied the troops dispatched to the North-West to put down the Métis rebellion. More nurses had served in South Africa and in the Great War, and in the

Second World War more than 50,000 women served in the Canadian Women's Army Corps (CWACs), the Women's Royal Canadian Naval Service (Wrens), and the Women's Division, Royal Canadian Air Force (WDs), filling a huge variety of non-combat roles. Thousands more served as nurses. After the Korean War, other military trades became open to women, and by the early 1970s, eighteen of twenty-seven officer classifications in the three services, and sixty-four of ninety-seven trades, had been declared gender-neutral. The quotas that had existed to control overall numbers of women service personnel disappeared in 1974, but women still accounted for only 3.6 percent of the regular force and 13.4 percent of the reserves. The numbers were rising, however, and more barriers were falling. The first twenty-four women cadets entered the Royal Military College in 1980, and twenty-one graduated as junior officers four years later. By every account, these initial female graduates were tougher and smarter than their male peers, and in 2002–3, 23.9 percent of RMC's enrolment were women.

The Charter increased the pressure on the last remaining barrier: the employment of women in combat and combat support positions. Curiously, quotas began to be reintroduced as a way of getting women into such posts. In 1986 the Chief of the Defence Staff created a special commission to examine the integration of women into combat roles, and a year later the army began its Combat Related Employment of Women (CREW) trials. By 1989 a Canadian Human Rights Tribunal chastised the military for the slow pace of gender integration and ordered that women be permitted to fill all military trades within a decade. One member of the tribunal, Colonel James Allan, disagreed with the majority of his colleagues, calling the decision "nonsensical . . . [for] trying to recruit women to the combat arms where most of them don't want to be." For whatever political reason, the government and the Canadian Forces had decided not to seek an exemption from the Charter of Rights and Freedoms. Now the forces had to pay the price.

Training standards for the army's combat arms had traditionally been high. Soldiers had to be tested in training so they could survive the stresses of battle. But women lack the upper body strength of men, and many potential women infanteers could not get through basic training. The standards were lowered to increase their chances, and a nineteen-year-old woman now had to meet the same standards as a forty-five-year-old male. "Which is okay," said Margaret Wente in the *Globe and Mail*, "so long as the enemy troops are all 45-year-old men." If anyone denied that standards had been lowered, one retired officer said, "That's a lie."*

141

---

*A Decima Research survey of CF personnel in June 2002 found that more than half of military personnel were overweight—an astonishing statistic. Some standards definitely were slipping.

This determination to include women in every role is a serious mistake. There are still many ways in which women can and should be accommodated in the Canadian Forces. Height requirements can be lowered and maternity leave provided on liberal terms. Spouses can be posted together to stop the break-up of families. It's also possible to root out whatever remains of the prejudices that, for example, kept women out of the pilot's seat on fighter jets far too long. But on the core roles of the military, there really cannot be a compromise of standards. A fit woman can fly a jet and have a good chance of surviving combat, but few women can lug heavy machine-guns and their belts of ammunition across country and fight enemy infantry. Some good sense might have saved the Canadian Forces from looking foolish—and hurting the achievement of future military missions.

Good sense was unfortunately in short supply in Ottawa. By December 1996 a de facto quota had been put in place and the army had been ordered to achieve "a critical mass of 25 percent women on future QL3 Combat Arms serials"—in other words, on the training of qualified infanteers.* The failure rate on courses stayed high, however, and, in 1998, studies conducted for the Chief of the Land Staff complained

---

*In military speak, the key sentence on training standards in the December 1996 order said: "Doctrine or practices that are incompatible with unrestricted participation [of designated groups, i.e., women] will be changed."

about "a male-dominated Combat Arms culture" that "pro-vided an unwelcome and overall non-supportive environ-ment for women." Appalling revelations in *Maclean's* that year about rapes and harassment of women in the Canadian Forces made clear just how "non-supportive" the atmos-phere could be.

The other environments also dealt with their own gender discrimination issues. The air force had aircrew of both gen-ders, including women CF-18 pilots, and navy ships sailed with mixed crews. In March 2001 the last barrier in the navy disappeared when the Chief of the Maritime Staff announced that women could serve on submarines. Norway, Sweden, and Australia had done it and, despite opposition from male sailors, Canada would as well. The equality provisions of Canadian law demanded no less.

While this policy of eliminating gender restrictions went on, the Canadian Forces lifted all barriers against gay and lesbian recruits. Before 1988, homosexuals had been barred from military service, though many had served quietly and were doing so still. The Charter and the *Canadian Human Rights Act* made any discrimination against gay personnel illegal, and the Canadian Forces adapted as best it could. The Chief of the Defence Staff said in 1992 that "inappropriate sexual conduct by members of the forces, whether heterosex-ual or homosexual," would not be tolerated. An academic study a decade later noted calmly that while this policy was

143

"not universally embraced," it "does appear to be universally accepted."

The integration of women into all military roles, however, was not universally embraced, but it, too, must become universally accepted. In my view, the task for the Canadian Forces is to find ways to bring substantial numbers of women into all parts of the armed forces and to make it work. The Israelis have done it, and the Americans are in the throes of integration just as Canada is. There will be difficulties and nasty incidents, but the military leadership must bring the die-hards into line. It may be that, in a war, the sight of women infanteers or sailors killed in action will lead to a reversal of policy, but until that time, the Canadian Forces has no choice but to persevere.

Even so, the utter silliness of the political correctness agenda is sometimes impossible to accept. The Canadian Forces in 2000 began setting rules that permitted men and women with disabilities to serve—with "a justifiable exemption" made by the Chief of the Defence Staff or by administrative review. Two years earlier, the CF policy had become one of "targets"—or quotas, in plain speech—for visible minorities. The aim was to enlist some 25 percent of recruits from non-white segments of the Canadian population in order to redress the 2-percent "vis min" representation current at the time and bring it as quickly as possible into line with the 9 percent of visible minorities in the national labour force. By the beginning of the new century, the Canadian Forces, labouring to satisfy the strictures of Ottawa's *Employment Equity Act*, had firmly fixed recruiting quotas in place: 28 percent women, 9 percent visible minorities, and 3 percent aboriginal peoples. The forces' poor harassed recruiters, of course, failed to achieve these quotas because a volunteer force cannot make people join. That didn't stop the Minister's Advisory Board on Canadian Forces Gender Integration and Employment Equity in 2001 from blaming this result on the military's culture "of insensitivity, ignorance and biases."

The ignorance was in the Advisory Board and in the government's policy of quotas. Both assumed that recruitment must discriminate against visible minorities, women, and aboriginals; otherwise, there would be more from these groups in the ranks. There is not a shred of evidence that this is so. The process is wrong, in the first place, because (like much other Canadian legislation) it is creating race-based thinking that would do Hitler proud. Quotas are simply wrong. In the second place, it neglects the reality that the new immigrants to Canada do not spread evenly across the country but concentrate in Toronto, Montreal, Vancouver, and Calgary, completely avoiding those parts of the Atlantic provinces from which present-day recruits come in large numbers. (One-fifth of the crew of HMCS *Fredericton* in 2003 was from Newfoundland and Labrador, for example, even though the province accounts for just over 2 percent of the population.) Third, the policy overlooks the fact that many of these new immigrants come to this country to escape military depredations against them, and it will take years before they are acculturated into our supposedly kinder and gentler ways and view the Canadian Forces as "a good thing." And, fourth, the policy of quotas makes clear that the Canadian government does not view its military as a fighting force that must be as efficient, effective, and well-trained as possible, but more as a social acculturation agency designed to replicate the Canadian population and make everyone welcome in shared tolerance and equality. An army of social workers may be a credible national goal, a reflection of our so-called and much-cherished societal values, but it remains to be proven that it will be effective in protecting Canada's national interests.

Many have doubts. Quotas are not the way to recruit a university faculty or a corporate workforce, and they are definitely not the way to recruit an army, navy, or air force. Quotas will lead to discrimination against those white males who do want to join the forces, to the acceptance of some recruits who manifestly should be rejected, to the continued lowering of training standards, and to a further weakening of public confidence in and support for the military. Journalist Donna Laframboise put it well: "An Armed Forces in which senior brass are expected to meet gender and skin colour quotas is one in which standards and morale are guaranteed to plummet." To me, that assessment is correct.

The entrenchment of political correctness in the Canadian Forces was not wholly the fault of the Mulroney government. The process began under Pierre Trudeau and continued under Jean Chrétien. What can be said is that the Conservatives did absolutely nothing to try to check the process. Because Mulroney was a Conservative and because soldiers, sailors, and airmen are generally conservative in their outlook,* the sense of betrayal under his government was greater than it might otherwise have been.

Let me be absolutely clear. I want women, aboriginal, and visible minority Canadians to join the Canadian Forces and to have the opportunity to take up every role and military trade they wish. Our laws direct this freedom, and I support them in this objective. We have enough history from the two world wars to know that a military that doesn't welcome all its citizens will get Canada into trouble. I believe it is critically important to this nation's future to make the Canadian Forces open to everyone—a true exercise in nation-building. But this openness does not mean gender or racial quotas, or

---

*Military personnel are not necessarily Progressive Conservative voters, however. Because military votes overseas are segregated and identifiable in the totals and because most CF bases have their own polling stations, it is possible to trace with limited accuracy how the military and military families have voted. The one academic study (by this author) showed that, to 1968, the CF consistently voted Liberal. No one has examined the elections since then.

the lowering of training requirements. We need to remember that the overriding purpose of the armed forces is to serve the national interest in ways that range from fighting wars to peacekeeping to the maintenance of domestic order. Our recruiting and our training cannot forget this objective. Setting recruiting quotas and lowering training standards to serve political and social goals is no favour to the nation, and race is surely the most inflammatory category around which to develop either a military or a society. The relentless racialist rhetoric of Canadian society—presented, of course, as multiculturalist anti-racism—is depressing enough without having to watch the Canadian Forces jump through hoops in an effort to satisfy the impossible quotas imposed on it.

The blame can more readily be fixed on the Mulroney government for the troubles that trapped the Canadian Forces, and especially the army, in Somalia. And those troubles began in Yugoslavia, where, in 1992, the United Nations established a peacekeeping force to try to stop Serbs, Croats, and Bosnians from killing each other as the nation broke up.

148

In Chapter 1, I raised the subject of peacekeeping and talked of Canadians' affection for the concept. Prime Minister Mulroney shared this belief in peacekeeping, and he was—or often tried to be—a good ally, a good global citizen. The Canadian Forces performed well in this role domestically too, as Mulroney discovered when Mohawks from Kanestake and Kahnawake in Quebec began armed protests over some municipal matters. Mulroney sent in the army when the Sûreté du Québec was unable to control matters. The 5e Brigade, based at Valcartier, did the job, enticing the Mohawk Warriors, illegally equipped with anti-tank weapons and sniper rifles, out of their trenches and defusing a tense situation in full view of the media. The army restored public order and civil authority.

When Yugoslavia fell apart after the death of its dictator, Josip Broz Tito, and the end of the Cold War, Mulroney confidently committed a battalion of infantry to UNPROFOR, the UN Protection Force, in the spring of 1992. Mulroney's wife's family is of Serbian origin, and the Mulroneys had honeymooned there. The battalion, taken from the small brigade in NATO, was a composite unit numbering 1,200 in all, dubbed Canbat I, put together from the Royal Canadian Regiment and the Royal 22e Régiment, the first time the Canadian Forces had been obliged to use such a process.*

UNPROFOR had a weak mandate and was signally

---

*Composite units violate one of the key principles of any military: unit cohesion. Soldiers fight not for lofty ideals but for their buddies. In good units, soldiers trust each other and their leaders. In bad units, they don't. The most recent study of this phenomenon is Leonard Wong et al., "Why They Fight: Combat Motivation in the Iraq War," published by the US Army War College Strategic Studies Institute at Carlisle, Pennsylvania, July 2003.

unable to stop all sides from mass killings at Sarajevo, Srebrenica, and countless other villages. The UN nonetheless created UNPROFOR II for Bosnia, its mandate limited to protecting humanitarian aid convoys. Canada provided a second battalion for this force, Canbat II, eventually upgrading its fighting capacity as all sides demonstrated they had no hesitation in attacking UNPROFOR troops. The Canadians, the second battalion of the Princess Patricia's Canadian Light Infantry, eventually fought in the Medak Pocket the largest battle the Canadian Forces had faced since Korea. There, in September 1993, they squared off successfully against heavily armed Croatian troops who were engaged in "ethnic cleansing," as late-twentieth-century genocide had come to be called. It took years before the public heard of this fight because the government and the Department of National Defence sat on the story. Canadians were peacekeepers, not warriors, after all, and if the public knew that Canadian soldiers had inflicted an estimated 27 deaths and 130 casualties on the Croatians without suffering any losses in action themselves, there might be trouble. The Princess Pats received a United Nations Force Commanders' Commendation, one of only three ever awarded, and in December 2002 Ottawa decorated them for their role in the pocket—a decade after the event.

The Canadian Forces performed its roles credibly enough in the former Yugoslavia and may even have felt better about the commitment as NATO became more enmeshed in that conflict. Nonetheless, the British complained that the Canadians' rules of engagement were so limited that they made Canbat I and II into almost ineffective units, the "Can'tbats."* The army was so under-strength and so over-committed that it could not easily sustain the commitment. At the time Canada joined UNPROFOR, the army's total personnel approximated 20,000. A small brigade was still in NATO, and Canada found itself with additional and rapidly expanding peacekeeping commitments as the UN rushed to fill the vacuum created by the end of the Cold War. Peoples and states that had been frightened into conformity by the superpowers suddenly felt free to settle old scores, and many did with a will.

The list of Canadian peacekeeping commitments in the early 1990s totalled forty-six missions in places such as Afghanistan, the Western Sahara, Cambodia, Nicaragua, and El Salvador. The smallest Canadian contingent was a single officer; the largest numbered 1,250. Most, but not all, of the Canadians came from the army. Most were combat

151

---

*Fen Hampson and Dean Oliver pointed out that it wasn't just the Canadians who had difficulties: "United Nations peacekeepers in Bosnia were repeatedly handcuffed by rules of engagement that generally prohibited the use of force against local warlords and by a pitiful weapons suite that would have rendered such bravado suicidal in any case." "Pulpit Diplomacy," *International Journal*, Summer 1998.

arms—infantry, armour, engineers, signals, artillery—and most, but not all, were regulars. Over time, the army's very small militia was asked to provide more and more junior ranks. In the Medak Pocket battle, for instance, the Princess Patricia's platoons were close to 70 percent reservists. They acquitted themselves very well in action.

This variety of UN commitments, added to the NATO obligation, which did not end until 1994, strained the army beyond endurance. Soldiers went on a deployment overseas for six months, returned home for six months, and were posted abroad again. The pressure this regime created for families was extreme. Service families lived in subsidized housing on military bases, but the rents kept increasing towards market rates and, too often, the housing was substandard. Frequent absences abroad strained marriages and short-changed children, and wife-beating, drunkenness, and divorce were common. Moreover, sometimes the trauma of UN service permanently scarred soldiers. Many of those who saw massacres in the former Yugoslavia or later in Rwanda were shattered by their experience, yet the military showed little ability or desire to help regulars and reservists suffering from post-traumatic stress disorder.

By the time Canada offered in August 1992 to provide troops for UNOSOM, the UN mission in a chaotic Somalia, the army was reeling under the strain, its commitments vastly exceeding its capabilities. The United States soon

152

stepped in to take the lead in the Unified Task Force, or UNITAF, an American-commanded force with a tougher mandate under Chapter VII of the UN Charter, and Mulroney wanted to assist his friend, President George Bush, when he called in November. As Grant Dawson wrote in his Carleton University doctoral dissertation, "Mulroney wanted to help Bush because his most important priority was the management of the Canada-US tie through personal diplomacy." Besides, what Canada did best was peace-keeping, right? So Canada agreed to join in, even though every available infantry battalion or armoured regiment in the army was on peacekeeping duty, just back from overseas, or preparing to go on yet another peacekeeping duty.

The sole available unit was the Canadian Airborne Regiment, the nation's UN standby battalion and a parachute-trained battalion with three commandos, each formed from one of the regular force regiments in the army—the Princess Patricia's, the Royal 22ᵉ Régiment, and the Royal Canadian Regiment. There were several points against its deployment in Somalia. Regimental cultures and languages were differ-ent. The Airborne, at its worst a classic example of the prob-lems a composite unit could face, had sometimes been a dumping ground for troublemakers. Moreover, just as the regiment was being forced to reorganize itself as a mecha-nized battalion for Somalia, its commanding officer had to be changed shortly before deployment. All these factors complicated its preparation and, when the original UN operation ceased and UNITAF took over, the regiment's training changed once more. The unit now had to ready itself for vigorous Article VII peacekeeping. At the same time, a Royal Canadian Dragoons armoured squadron, borrowing vehicles and parts from other units, joined the contingent to give it more punch. Despite these potential problems with the Canadian Airborne, the military sent Colonel Serge Labbé, the contingent commander, to see the general in command of UNITAF and ask for a major role for the regiment. He got it. The rules of engagement were not well understood by the soldiers, however, and, when the tour of service was extended, the delay in patriation hurt morale. Meanwhile, Labbé had his headquarters in Mogadishu, hundreds of kilometres away. In the confusion, the troubles that befell the Canadian Airborne Regiment were almost predictable.

Stationed in Belet Uen, the regiment lived in tents in the sand, ate from US ration packs (because Ottawa had refused to send a field kitchen), and came to dislike the Somalis, who, the soldiers believed, tried to steal everything that wasn't nailed down. Subsequent studies demonstrated that racism was prevalent in every national force participating in the Somalia operation, not least the American, Italian, and Belgian. The troops did their duty, nonetheless, impressed their US commanders, and, overall, made a positive impact on a troubled country.

154

Unfortunately, tragically, some members of the regiment tortured and killed a Somali youth on March 16, 1993, while others, including warrant officers, heard screams and inexplicably did nothing, indicating either a complete collapse of discipline or, just as likely, fear of their own soldiers among the officers. Once the crime was known, officers covered up parts of the mess in a chain extending from Somalia to various levels at National Defence Headquarters in Ottawa. The object seemed to be to protect the regiment, the army, senior officers, and Kim Campbell, the Minister of National Defence, who was then running for the Progressive Conservative Party leadership and the succession to Brian Mulroney as Prime Minister. As the historian of the Canadian Airborne noted, "a conscious decision was made to control any political damage rather than see public justice done." It was a historic error.

There is another factor here that reflects directly on the Canadian Forces' leadership. In 1989 National Defence Headquarters had prepared a plan to deploy a task force to Haiti, a scheme allegedly so inept that operational commanders refused to let it proceed. In the end, the operation was cancelled for other reasons, but the Chief of the Defence Staff ordered a study of the role of headquarters in emergencies. The findings were clear and damning. The command responsibilities of the military and National Defence Headquarters had been compromised by the 1972 amalgamation of the military and civilian headquarters; the

155

responsibilities for command and control were diffuse and confused; and the Canadian Forces had no strategic concept. National Defence Headquarters should not try to command operations in the field.

The result of these conclusions was the creation of headquarters' Joint Staff, or J Staff, which began to function in 1990 and made an effort to give the Canadian Forces a sense of collective purpose. In 1992–93 the J Staff was still finding its feet. Thus, the Canadian Forces continued to rely on the good training of units and the common sense of their commanding officers to save it in difficult situations. This confidence usually worked, because units were generally well trained and the commanders capable. In Somalia, however, a weak commanding officer, a troubled unit, and confused planning at the top all came together.

If the Canadian Forces had told the Prime Minister that Somalia was one peacekeeping operation too many, a host of troubles and tragedies might have been avoided. But the generals knew that Mulroney was an activist, hands-on Prime Minister, keen on peacekeeping. They knew, as well, that one of his government's goals was to get the United States as involved in multilateral operations as possible. The Prime Minister was taking media heat because of the coverage of horrors in Somalia, and Canadians were asking why their forces had troops in the former Yugoslavia ("a rich man's war") and not in Somalia. Under the circumstances, instead

156

of complaining, the generals said "Yes, Sir," and set out to make the operation happen as best they could. That turned out to be not good enough.

There is little point here in detailing the rest of the Somalia and Canadian Airborne debacle. Video evidence of racist behaviour, vile hazing rituals, and other unpleasant actions eventually emerged in January 1995 and horrified the country when they were screened on TV.* The gung-ho, macho style of the Canadian Airborne seemed profoundly un-Canadian, and the public, Parliament, and media saw this discrepancy at once. Our boys, carrying our values, were running amok, or so journalist Peter Desbarats put it. The Canadian way of war—and peacekeeping—did not encompass tattoos, Confederate flags, and racial sneers and killings. So sharp was the reaction that the Liberal government was all but forced to disband the regiment in late January 1995 in an effort to stop the rising tide of criticism from washing over the Canadian Forces, the army, and the regimental system. The Chrétien government created a Commission of Inquiry in March 1995 to investigate what had gone wrong in Somalia, but the commission, headed by a sputtering and splenetic judge, unaccountably lost its way and began investigating alterations to

*The Airborne's rituals are the subject of academic study. See sociologist Donna Winslow, "Rites of Passage and Group Bonding in the Canadian Airborne," a paper presented to the American Sociological Association, 1997.

press releases rather than the central issues. In January 1997, before its work was finished, Doug Young, the Liberal Defence Minister, ordered it to shut down at the end of March and to submit its report in June.

What had gone wrong in the army and at National Defence Headquarters? Clearly there were serious problems in the Airborne Regiment. Where were the sergeants and the officers? Why didn't they intervene to stop the torture that March night in Belet Uen? Were they intimidated by their troopers? Their inaction suggested a complete and wilful breakdown in authority and discipline, and the videos provided yet more evidence of this kind. The cover-up suggested rampant careerism among some senior officers and senior civilian bureaucrats in the Department of National Defence and too acute a sensitivity to the political needs of the Minister. The report of the Somalia commission, appallingly titled *Dishonoured Legacy*, made some of these points, though it was far too eager to blame a few individuals in the military.

At root, the cause of the Somalia affair was the government's inability to say no. Canadian leaders loved the kudos they received in Washington and New York for ponying up troops for UN and other service. They enjoyed the favourable editorials praising their devotion to peacekeeping, and opinion polls confirmed that the electorate liked it too. The senior leadership may have pointed to the strains on its troops as the Canadian Forces tried to mount one overseas operation after another, but, when pressed by the Prime Minister, the Defence Minister, and the Deputy Minister, the generals and admirals invariably saluted and said "can do." Their training, their ethos, left them little option. The men might be tired and their units under-strength, the training might not always be adequate, and the equipment might be obsolete, but, by God, the politicians and generals were ready, aye ready. As a result, the Commission of Inquiry correctly pointed out, the Canadians arrived in Somalia "with an uncertain mission, unknown task, ad hoc command arrangements, an unconsolidated relationship to U.S. command, and unclear rules of engagement." There ought to have been no surprise that an overstretched military, with all ranks under stress, plunged into a morass.

A few generals certainly merit a full share of the blame for the disaster that tarnished the Canadian Forces. But, ultimately, the country's political leadership must take responsibility for the ruination of the Canadian Forces in the 1990s. It was Prime Minister Mulroney who agreed to commitment after commitment while failing to ensure that the forces had the necessary manpower, the funds, the equipment, and the training to do the jobs they were being asked to undertake. Indeed, Mulroney sent Canadians to the former Yugoslavia and Somalia at precisely the time he was cutting the forces' strength and reducing the number of battalion-sized units. Who killed the Canadian military? Brian Mulroney did.

159

CHAPTER 6

Last Rites:
Jean Chrétien Finishes Off
the Canadian Forces

WHO killed the Canadian military? Jean Chrétien won three majority victories, battled the country's deficit to the ground, and helped to elect a Liberal and anti-separatist government in Quebec through his tough federalist policies. Those achievements were real and important, and they may yet see him called a great Prime Minister once present passions have cooled and historians have perspective on events. But the historians of the future should also remember that Chrétien was the leader who reduced the Canadian Forces to an effective strength just above 50,000 and, by accepting commitment after commitment, exacerbated the burnout of soldiers, sailors, and aircrew. Chrétien was the Prime Minister who slashed the defence budget to the bone, dithered shamefully on military cooperation with the United States in a time of crisis, and delayed and stalled major equipment purchases in the years of global terrorism and war. This record is not the stuff of greatness. Who finished off the Canadian Forces? Jean Chrétien did.

* * *

The event that set the tone for the new Liberal government's attitude to the military came within days of Jean Chrétien's arrival at 22 Sussex Drive. Brian Mulroney's Progressive Conservative government had placed an order for EH-101 Cormorant helicopters for use on Canadian destroyers and frigates and in search and rescue operations, replacing the thirty-two 30-year-old Sea King and fifteen Labrador helicopters. Chrétien cancelled the contract for what he called "Cadillac" helicopters outright, committing the government to pay a cancellation fee of almost half a billion dollars.

No one disagreed that a new helicopter was essential, probably not even Chrétien. The shipborne copters worked on anti-submarine warfare duties, on surveillance, on transporting personnel and supplies between ships and from ship to shore, and on search and rescue duties at sea. The search and rescue work at home largely took place over Canada's waters, internal and off-shore. These roles were already in jeopardy because of the equipment limitations, a problem the cancellation now worsened dramatically by delaying the date of delivery. The Chrétien government's White Paper of 1994 noted dryly: "There is an urgent need for robust and capable new shipborne helicopters. The Sea Kings are rapidly approaching the end of their operational life." It committed the government to "identify options and plans to put into service new affordable replacement helicopters by the end of the decade." Although fifteen helicopters (an EH-101 variant also called Cormorants) ordered in 1998 to serve in search and rescue roles came into service five years later, the procurement process for a Sea King replacement, hampered at every turn by political meddling, had gone nowhere ten years after the EH-101 cancellation.

The now forty-year-old Sea Kings continued to fly from Canadian naval vessels, each hour of flying operations requiring countless hours of maintenance work and jeopardizing both their missions and the safety of their crews. Assuming that a contract for new helicopters is let under Chrétien's successor, Paul Martin, it will be at least 2009 before they come into service in the navy. Whether the new machine will be or even should be as capable as the EH-101 of 1993 is in dispute among helicopter manufacturers, the Canadian Forces, and the government. Except for the politicians, everyone agrees that the delay has been shameful, dangerous to personnel, and a sure indicator of the priorities of the government. Without doubt, defence ranked very low for Chrétien's administration.

What mattered to the Liberal government were the budget deficit and the national debt. "The accumulated debt of the federal and provincial governments currently stands at approximately $750 billion," the White Paper stipulated, and "the federal government's annual debt servicing payments in 1994–95 alone will amount to $44 billion—more than the budget deficit of $39.7 billion and some 27 percent of the total federal budget." The situation was genuinely serious, and the Canadian Forces had to carry its share. The White Paper, however, made clear that defence spending over the next half-dozen years would be "less than 60 percent of that assumed in the 1987 Defence White Paper." The National Defence budget fell, in constant 1992–93 dollars, from $11.8 billion when the Liberals took power to $9.5 billion four years later. The budget cuts were reflected most sharply in the strength of the Canadian Forces. From manpower strengths of 126,000 in 1962, 88,000 in 1989, and 75,900 in 1994, the number was projected to fall to 60,000 officers and non-commissioned members by 1999. This commitment, at least, was one the Chrétien government would keep. Indeed, the government would do more than meet this pledge.

I can understand the government's motivation. The debt was large and growing and it threatened the credit of the nation. Every department was being slashed, and even programs that had long been seen as sacred were dismantled. Defence spending could not be immune. The White Paper pledged, however, that Canada would not allow its military to sink to the level of a constabulary, for the "maintenance of multi-purpose, combat-capable forces is in the national interest." Yet how was it possible to maintain combat-capable forces with dwindling numbers, operating with obsolete equipment, on a shrinking budget? If the promise of budget cuts was scrupulously kept, the pledge to maintain real military strength would dissolve.

Compounding matters was the government's refusal to say no to requests for overseas deployments. Like Mulroney before him, Chrétien loved the idea of sending Canadian troops abroad. The 1994 White Paper, while pronouncing "multilateral security cooperation" as "the expression of Canadian values in the international sphere," also suggested that some requirements should be met before Canadian troops were committed. There should be a clear, enforceable mandate and an identifiable reporting authority. The composition of the force should be appropriate, and the consultation process among members effective. Moreover, Canadian participation should be accepted by all parties to the conflict; the size, training, and equipment of any Canadian force should be right for the mission; and a defined concept of operations, effective command and control, and clear rules of engagement should be mandatory to determine when and how Canadian soldiers could use force. These requirements were not only correct but similar to those defined by Lester Pearson in 1956 and by successive governments. Unfortunately, they would not always be honoured.

The Liberals brought back the Canadian brigade and air group from NATO, in keeping with the decision made by the Mulroney government, as well as the Canadian Airborne

167

Regiment from Somalia. The thirty-year participation in the UN Force in Cyprus finally ended in 1994. Rightly or wrongly, that closed out three overseas commitments. The government thereupon increased the commitment to the former Yugoslavia, sending a brigade headquarters and even more troops, over 1,000 all told, to serve with the NATO Implementation Force in late 1995. When NATO changed the name of its peacemaking operation to the Stabilization Force the next year, Canada increased its commitment to more than 1,200 soldiers. Then, in 1999, Canada provided more than 1,300 troops to NATO's Kosovo Force. With the exception of a part-squadron of CF-18s (for which the government had to scramble to find precision-guided munitions), almost all the troops came from the army. These deployments were a major strain on Canada's shrinking, over-stretched land forces.

There was more. In 1996 the Canadian government sent forces to Haiti, cooperating with the United States in an effort to stabilize that island nation (and also to stop a flood of refugees heading for Florida).* The army provided a commander, Major-General Roméo Dallaire, and some staff

168

---

*At a NATO leaders meeting in July 1997, Chrétien was overheard explaining how he had agreed to the Haiti commitment during a conversation with US President Bill Clinton: "So he calls me, okay. I send my soldiers. Thank you very much, but later I ask for something in return."

officers for an undermanned, ill-equipped UN force in
Rwanda, one that proved utterly incapable of stopping one
of the most horrific genocides of recent years. The government also sent General Maurice Baril that year to scout out
the situation in the Democratic Republic of the Congo. The
Prime Minister had seen the killings, chaos, and hunger
there on television and, some journalists speculated, he
knew that a mission to francophone Africa would play well
in Quebec. The proposed operation ended in confusion and
disarray because Canada had little hard intelligence data on
either the area or the situation and soon proved itself
incapable of mounting, leading, or supplying a major
peacekeeping/humanitarian mission. An in-house military
study of this botched affair, written the next year, bluntly
observed that "the CF, particularly at the National Defence
Headquarters level, uses planning and mounting procedures
for operations which often do not get the job done effectively because they are improperly applied." There was, the
report went on, "systemic inability" to organize swiftly for
emergency deployments, notwithstanding the establishment
a half-dozen years earlier of the Joint Staff. The "bungle in
the jungle," the troops called this fiasco. "It's like they
learned nothing from Somalia," one retired senior officer
said. "Here we were going off, once again, to a place where
no-one wanted us, with an attitude of don't worry, we know
what's best for you." The only truly credible explanation,

others said, was a shameless seeking after Nobel Peace Prizes by the Prime Minister and his Foreign Minister, and *Saturday Night* ran an article about the whole exercise under the title "Nobel Fever."

Canada sent a reinforced company to UNMEE, the UN Mission in Ethiopia and Eritrea, in 2000–1, and maintained more than two hundred troops on the Golan Heights, trying to keep the peace between Israel and Syria. There were, in addition, other UN commitments ranging across the continents that had to be met. Complicating everything was the fact that UN missions were no longer only peacekeeping but now included peace enforcement. In other words, the troops in blue helmets were no longer impartial observers; they could and would fight if necessary to impose their will. That required different training, weaponry, and equipment and increased the risk of casualties.

After the terrorist attacks of September 11, 2001, Chrétien's Canada rightly joined in the War on Terrorism. A large part of the navy's fleet served in the area, playing a role in regulating ship traffic and searching for terrorists. The air force based Hercules aircraft in the region, ferrying supplies and personnel. And National Defence Headquarters dispatched the 3rd Princess Patricia's Canadian Light Infantry and a squadron of Lord Strathcona's Horse to serve in Afghanistan. The soldiers performed well, though a company of infantry had to be added from another battalion of the PPCLI to bring the 3rd Battalion up to strength. There were other problems: the troops had to be flown to the theatre on borrowed aircraft; they had to use ground and helicopter transport provided by the US forces; and they had the wrong uniforms for desert terrain and the wrong boots, always an important matter to foot-slogging infantry. Canadian snipers demonstrated their highly specialized skills to good effect, however, and some forty members of the Canadian special forces from the secret (and unnecessarily secretive) JTF-2 also served. But the death of four Princess Patricia's soldiers, when a United States Air Force jet mistakenly bombed a night live-firing exercise, unfortunately became the defining moment of the operation and sparked a burst of anti-American sentiment in Canada.

The difficulty for the Canadian Forces was that it could not maintain the operational tempo the government set. In 1999, before the Afghan operation, Canada had some 4,500 troops abroad, or some 7 percent of the forces' nominal strength of 60,000 and 8.25 percent of its actual trained strength of just under 54,000. Most were army personnel, and the overseas commitments amounted to approximately 20 percent of the army's total strength. The stressful pace continued. At the beginning of 2002 the Canadian Forces had 1,600 troops in Bosnia and more than 2,500 in Operation Apollo, the Afghanistan mission. At that point the army decided it could not replace the Princess Patricia's in

Afghanistan after its six-month tour—no other battle group could be posted to the war against the Taliban and al-Qaeda. At the same time, the air force's Hercules C-130 transports in the Middle East began to have serious mechanical problems, and the crews and technicians were stretched very thin in the effort to keep the old aircraft flying.

The navy, too, was reaching the breaking point. Its ability to keep its destroyers and frigates at sea was flagging and, at the end of June 2003, the navy announced that it had to "pause." After sending sixteen of its eighteen ships and 97 percent of its sea-going personnel to the Persian Gulf since the beginning of the War on Terrorism in late 2001, it could not take on any additional operations abroad. The east coast fleet, its commander said, would devote its efforts to maintenance and to upgrading electronics "on this side of the Atlantic." The navy, added Admiral Ron Buck, the Chief of the Maritime Staff, will "rest, re-generate and rebuild, and look after our people."

The army likely wished it could do the same after years of wearing itself out in the effort to sustain its commitments in Bosnia. Instead, in its successful effort to avoid sending troops to fight with the United States and Britain in the war against Saddam Hussein's Iraq in 2003, the Chrétien government dispatched a brigade headquarters and troops to Afghanistan in Operation Athena, to work with a UN-authorized but (from August 2003) NATO-run International

Security Assistance Force (ISAF) in Kabul. What the army contingent was to do there, beyond patrolling the dangerous streets of Kabul, and which Canadian national interest this deployment served remain a mystery, unexplained by the government. Nonetheless, some 2,000 troops (including a major-general, a brigadier-general, one colonel and two lieutenant-colonels, and, once Canada takes command of ISAF in 2004, a lieutenant-general) were involved in protecting Hamid Karzai's regime against the warlords and Taliban forces opposing it. The government planned to rotate the troops home in six months and replace them with other soldiers from Canada. Canada's tiny army was providing 40 percent of the Kabul force in an increasingly tense nation, as the Americans on the ground were still fighting Taliban irregulars and seeking out al-Qaeda remnants. By October 2003 NATO had won the UN Security Council's unanimous approval to expand its writ into the rest of Afghanistan, a task estimated to require up to 10,000 more alliance troops.

Whatever this operation was, it wasn't peacekeeping, said the commanding officer of the 2nd Royal Canadian Regiment battle group in Kabul, his command equipped with vigorous rules of engagement and including Royal Canadian Dragoons Coyote reconnaissance vehicles, a battery of 105-mm artillery, and four newly purchased ($34 million) French-made unmanned aerial vehicles (or spy drones). "God, I hate it when they call us peacekeepers. We loathe the term, abhor it. Peacekeeping," said Lieutenant-Colonel Don Denne, "can turn into a general war situation in the snap of your fingers." Dr. Sean Maloney, a leading peacekeeping scholar, noted: "If we get out of there with no casualties, we'll be lucky."* The international force had under 5,000 soldiers, there were 27,000 fighters loyal to various warlords in the city, and Taliban recruits were nearby as well. "If fighting breaks out," Maloney said, "ISAF troops will find it almost impossible to control a city with a population exceeding 2 million." If that occurred, the peace enforcement nature of ISAF would become apparent to all.

Compounding matters as I write, almost 250 civilian contractors, about half Canadian and the rest Nepalese, Indians, Pakistanis, and nationals from other countries, have been hired to supply and service the Canadians. Civilians are cheaper than using soldiers that Canada's shrunken army logistic system doesn't have, so luck might be needed to keep the troops sustained in the event of major difficulties. The

---

*We would not be lucky. On October 2, 2003, two Canadian soldiers were killed and three wounded in a presumed land mine explosion that destroyed an Iltis patrol vehicle. Ottawa scrambled to find sixteen more armoured vehicles to send to Kabul. The Canadian troops there had thirty but needed sixty more. They would make do with the additional sixteen. When he was asked if, as the Minister had said, no effort had been spared to get the contingent everything it needed, Lieutenant-Colonel Don Denne, commander of the Royal Canadian Regiment battle group, replied eloquently, "Boy, that's a road I don't really want to go down."

contractors (who include a Canadian grandmother who is a kitchen supervisor) are untrained, unarmed, and only nominally subject to military discipline, and, as such, they constitute a dangerous liability for the Canadians in Operation Athena. Until Afghanistan, the Canadian Forces had always declared that the use of civilian contractors was intended for "mature/stable/and benign theatres."* We can only hope that the Kabul mission will be benign and stable, but if the worst occurs, the Canadian commander in his headquarters at Camp Julien will have 250 civilian employees within his lines. The dangers should be obvious, even to the government that dispatched Canadians to Afghanistan.

The Afghan deployment, besides being risky, will stretch the army's already tight manpower situation to its limit and cost an estimated $900 million. "Do we want to make a difference," asked the retiring Chief of the Land Staff in May 2003, "or do we just want to ensure our diplomatic presence?" The answer to that rhetorical question was not in doubt. Still, as historian Mark Proudman wrote, it was "a neat solution to a political problem." It was a contribution to the War against Terrorism but also one that "used up pretty well all our deployable forces, so we cannot now be

---

*CDS General Maurice Baril said in 2000: "Deciding that we are going to have contractors run many of our services in Bosnia is something that kind of makes you shake a little bit at night because it has never been done that way. . . . But our business is risk-taking."

asked to do more." General Raymond Henault, the Chief of Defence Staff, held that view, too. In a speech in Ottawa in September 2003, he said that when the land forces' Kabul commitment ended in the summer of 2004, the army would need eighteen months without a significant overseas deployment for recuperation.

A period of recovery time was desperately needed. Short of funds and personnel,* forced continually to ready itself for deployment, the army had all but stopped training at a high level. Only subunits—companies or squadrons—did extensive training. Training at the battle group level (ordinarily, an infantry battalion with attached engineer, combat support, and administrative subunits) took place solely in preparation for deployment to Bosnia or Afghanistan. The first brigade exercise in more than a decade was held in the spring of 2003 at Wainwright, Alberta, the result of special efforts to hoard funds and equipment by the Chief of the Land Staff, Lieutenant-General Mike Jeffrey. As a result of this dismal

---

176

*There were indications in late 2003 that Defence Minister John McCallum had become aware of the army's problems. In an interview on October 22 in the *Globe and Mail*, he indicated plans to spend more on the land forces, notably for new armoured vehicles, and possibly even an increase in army strength. The money apparently was to come from $130 million in savings at headquarters, but the armoured vehicles were projected to cost $600 million. Whether the Chrétien or the incoming Paul Martin government would buy into this idea was unclear.

record, almost all the present cadre of senior officers have no command experience in the field; if Canada had to fight a war, we would be in precisely the same position we were in 1914 and in 1939, with raw commanders leading partially trained and ill-equipped troops into battle. According to General Jeffrey, "Our collective skills have now eroded to a level that I have real concerns we can't get them back."

Even with three brigades in Canada, the army is unprepared to meet a crisis. Instead of being fighting formations, the brigades have become static headquarters, absorbed with the daily administration of garbage pickups at base and leave rosters. There are no regular army units in five of the provinces or in the North, where the army presence is limited to the very thin ranks of the militia. In British Columbia, where earthquakes, floods, and major forest fires are certain to occur, this absence has the potential for tragedy. Elsewhere, no matter how most Canadians try to pretend otherwise, all of Canada is subject to terrorist attacks, possibly with weapons of mass destruction. Because Canada is situated next to the United States, because Canada is secular, democratic, and capitalist, it is an inviting target to all who hate the West.

The army's militia is the Canadian Forces' first responder to domestic crises. But it is spread sparsely across the country, its strength is scheduled to rise only slowly towards 17,000 (in August 2003, militia paid strength was 12,023), its equipment is lacking, and, with a huge annual turnover rate of at least 25 percent, its training is not always adequate. The reserves, however, continue to provide junior ranks for overseas deployments, and militia soldiers have performed and continue to perform well. The army had to raid reserve units to fill the ranks, a sure indication that the band of personnel had been stretched too thin for too long.

The Canadian Forces had reached its breaking point. The soldiers and sailors were either deployed in the field, recuperating from a deployment, or preparing to be deployed. There was no respite, no time for training, no opportunity for reflection. Marriages suffered the strain of repeated separations, and children grew up in the absence of their fathers or their mothers (and in a few cases, the simultaneous absence of both on overseas deployments). The Chrétien government did not give a damn. It apparently considered that the superpower United States was so dominant, its military so clearly the technological leader on the new global battlefields created by the revolution in military affairs, that Canada could not possibly compete or pay the bills. So why bother? Peacekeeping required little high-tech weaponry, so send in the boys and girls with their outdated small arms. When Chrétien dispatched Canadian troops to a United Nations operation in East Timor in September 1999, he said guilelessly: "We're always there, like Boy Scouts, somewhat.

We're happy and Canadians love it. They think it's a nice way for Canadians to be present around the world."*

A similar record applies to operations in aid of the civil power. Fighting floods in Manitoba or ice storms in Quebec required rowboats, ropes, and ladders, much like the equipment of Boy Scouts or Sea Scouts, not the military weaponry required to fight a first-class enemy or even guerrillas. The attitude that the Prime Minister exhibited in October 1993 when he cancelled the helicopter contract remained unaltered throughout his administration. No Cadillacs, in other words, but unfortunately no Volkswagens either.

This charge is serious, but it is undeniable. Canada's military expenditure as a percentage of gross domestic product was, Luxembourg aside, the lowest in NATO, just 1.1 percent. The NATO average is 2.2 percent. The United States spends 3.2 percent of GDP on its military and, in 2004, this percentage amounts to a defence budget of US$380 billion—or well above $500 billion Canadian. Australia, a nation of 19 million people, today spends 1.9 percent of GDP on defence, some $14.4 billion Canadian, and has committed itself to a $47 billion defence capital expenditure over the next decade.

179

---

*"In Washington," said Michael Ignatieff in an address to the Institute for Public Affairs in Montreal on February 15, 2003, "I live my working life in a policy environment in which Canada is a kind of well-meaning Boy Scout. We are not taken seriously." Exactly.

Defence as a percentage of Canadian government expenditure was, at 8 percent, one-fifth of what it had been in 1954, and about half what it had been when Trudeau came to power in 1968. Defence expenditures in 2004, including the increase of $800 million for each of the next three years in the February 2003 budget, were just above $12 billion. But 25 percent of the budget for the Department of National Defence is spent in areas other than operational capability: pension contributions, environmental cleanups, and military support to provincial governments in natural disasters, to list a few examples. Only $3 billion of the DND budget went directly to the army, navy, and air force, and the navy, for example, received only $7 million more from the budget increase announced in 2003. The overall DND increase, while a start and a small triumph for Defence Minister John McCallum, was hardly enough to counter the 30-percent decrease in purchasing power that the Progressive Conservative and Liberal budget cuts had inflicted.

The strength of the Canadian Forces at the beginning of 2004 was nominally 60,000 all ranks, but in terms of trained personnel it was at least 7,000 fewer, taking into account those beginning training, those on disability leave, and those on leave before retirement. The navy's strength was just over 8,000 officers and ratings, with 4,100 in sea-going operations. Considering its tiny size, the navy has made a disproportionate contribution to the country's military efforts in the War on Terrorism, with more than 3,982 of its 4,100 sea-going sailors serving or having served in the Persian Gulf and the Arabian Sea. The air force's strength was 12,500, while the army counted 19,300. The remainder consisted of the purple trades, the unified support services of the Canadian Forces.

Even maintaining that attenuated strength was a challenge. The military's demographic profile was unfavourable, with thousands who had joined in the late 1960s, 1970s, and early 1980s nearing mandatory retirement age or the completion of twenty years' service, after which they could retire with a pension. Many of these CF members were the highly skilled technicians and the middle-rank officers on whom the forces' competence and professionalism depended; many more were senior non-commissioned members and officers getting out because they were angry with their government's lack of defence policy. At the same time, many of the new recruits, more than 10,000 of whom were attracted to the regular and reserve forces by a major advertising campaign in 2001–2 and 2002–3, were piled up doing meaningless chores in holding platoons at Camp Borden and other bases, waiting for space to open up in trades training courses. Simultaneously, the air force, which a decade before had launched a Force Reduction Plan to cut its pilot numbers and, in 2001, had a huge list of pilot trainees waiting for space at flying school, discovered in mid-2003 that it was under-strength, with only 845 pilots listed in flying jobs. In 2002, in fact, the air force could recruit only 48 pilot-trainees, although it had been looking for 184. HR (Mil), the Canadian Forces Human Resources operation, needed a serious shake-up.

And what of equipment? Much of the CF's kit is reaching "rust-out." When a family car has been driven into the ground, the cost of maintenance each year grows higher and the technological currency further erodes. For families, this comparison doesn't matter very much, except that the expenses keep rising. For the armed forces, however, for an army, navy, or air force that must contemplate fighting with or against another military with technologically advanced equipment, the problem is very different. As Colonel Brian MacDonald, a retired militia officer noted, "the military technological capabilities of allies and adversaries continues to advance and leaves stranded technology increasingly out of date and dangerous to its crew's survival in battle."

This situation is deadly serious for the Canadian military. Personnel costs, some 40 percent of budget now that the Canadian Forces has shrunk, and operations and maintenance (O&M) swallow almost 90 percent of the forces' budget, leaving little money for new equipment purchases or the renewal of existing equipment. The equipment budget in 1990 (many years after the peak of the nation's military expenditure) was $3.5 billion in 2001 dollars, but the capital budget in 2001 was only $1.3 billion. The shortfall is great on a year-to-year basis, but it is massive if Canada is ever to buy the equipment its navy, army, and air force will need to meet the challenges of warfare in the twenty-first century.

Consider the navy. Its destroyers were built in the early 1970s and modernized in the early 1990s. Their service life is nearing an end and, if they are not replaced or their command and control capacities not grafted onto a frigate or three, the navy's ability to run task groups at sea will be lost. This weakness will hit directly at the inter-operability of the Canadian navy with allied fleets, especially the United States Navy. The navy's two operational support ships (AORs), commissioned in 1969–70, are long past their "sell by" dates and should be replaced by ships that can support the fleet and army deployments abroad. If they are not, the navy will be unable to operate far from Canada for long unless supplies can be borrowed from allies, while the army will be forced to rely on chartered vessels. There is no Canadian shipyard that can now build new destroyers, support ships, or frigates, as the last, the Irving yard in Saint John, shut down for want of orders in 2003. Most of the seaworthy hulls need work. The navy's twelve frigates are first-class vessels built in the 1980s and 1990s, but they need to begin expensive mid-life upgrades within the next five years. The four British-built Victoria Class submarines, purchased from the Royal Navy in 1998 for a bargain-basement price of

$750 million (about one-quarter the cost of building new submarines), had their teething troubles much exaggerated in the media. They are now coming into service and will be capable vessels for the next twenty years. Their anti-submarine capacity (along with that of the frigates) is still needed, for many potentially hostile states are investing in submarines. The navy's twelve Maritime Coastal Defence Vessels, versatile little craft commissioned in the late 1990s and used primarily by the Naval Reserve, are useful in limited in-shore roles—and will remain so for another fifteen years. One of the four destroyers, HMCS *Huron*, tied up at Esquimalt since October 2000 for want of a crew, has now been officially taken out of service. The navy, which has been the best led and best equipped of the Canadian services, is now on the cusp of slipping into irrelevance and being reduced to a tiny coastal defence force.

The air force in 2003 numbers 15,000, its smallest strength since 1948. It flies 328 aircraft (which includes twenty-four ancient T33s, fifteen Labrador search and rescue helicopters already replaced by Cormorants, and ninety-nine Griffon helicopters, militarized versions of a commercial machine, which fly with the army), compared with the 3,826 aircraft it flew in 1966 (when it had a strength of 46,000 all ranks). Its CF-18 fighters on "air domination" duties now number only sixty in four front-line squadrons, and only one or two have yet received $10-million upgrades (in an "Omnibus CF-18

Incremental Modernization Project") to their sensors, computers, weapons, and communications equipment. Until they are all upgraded by a projected date of 2009, the fighters cannot readily be employed in cooperation with the more sophisticated US Air Force; even then, they will not be able to operate against the most advanced air or ground defences. The upgraded CF-18s are now expected to be employed, as Air Command in Winnipeg said in 2003, for "at least fifteen more years." The air force has had no air-to-air refuelling capacity since 1996, though two Airbus 310 Polaris aircraft are being modified to meet this need and are expected to be operational in 2004. The maritime patrol fleet of Aurora aircraft has shrunk from twenty-four to sixteen, and urgent modifications on the remaining aircraft, begun in 1999, have now been delayed to 2009 because of funding problems. Even with these modifications, the life of the Aurora airframes and electronics will run out by 2010 unless there are major structural upgrades. As it now stands, three to five Auroras are out of commission at any time; three are undergoing major inspection and repair; and two are receiving periodic maintenance. Only two to four Auroras on each of the coasts are ordinarily available for duty, and flying hours are dropping year by year. In September 2003 National Defence Headquarters indicated it was looking for a private company to do off-shore patrols. So much for the protection of Canadian sovereignty. Perhaps the American military could do the job for Ottawa.

There are more serious problems yet. Two-thirds of the thirty-two CC-130 Hercules aircraft, the air force's workhorse medium-range transport, were grounded in mid-2003 because of cracks in the airframe—perhaps not surprising, since nineteen of them are almost forty years old. The remaining thirteen aircraft were overcommitted, as five, for example, were based in the Persian Gulf to support the Canadian deployment in Afghanistan and French peacekeepers in the Democratic Republic of the Congo. All the Hercules, like the Sea Kings, required hugely expensive maintenance to keep them in the air: their unreliability forced the Canadian Forces to charter transports at premium prices and to search for old airframes it could cannibalize; and both maintenance and charter costs ate deeply into the defence budget. The lack of trained crews, the scarcity of experienced maintenance technicians, and the shortage of armament "suites," which are essential when flying in potential war zones, all hampered the air force. The Hercules need to be replaced*—new C-130Js sell for an estimated $200 million each—and there is, in addition, pressure for long-range air transport like the American C-17. In the event of an emergency, the old Hercules (which can carry only ninety troops at a time) could not, for instance, readily extricate the Canadian contingent in Kabul, Afghanistan.

---

*Defence Minister McCallum has indicated that Canada will "likely" acquire more Hercules transport aircraft in the medium term.

The army has some first-rate equipment, notably its Coyote reconnaissance and its LAV-III armoured wheeled vehicles, but Defence Minister McCallum decided in 2003 to eliminate its tanks, Leopards purchased by Trudeau from Germany in the late 1970s and recently upgraded. The government is also now upgrading the fleet of forty-year-old MII3 armoured personnel carriers, fitting them for behind-the-lines roles. The army's Griffon helicopters have limited lift capacity, are under-armed, and, at best, might barely cope in "mid-intensity" conflict—if Canada has allies on whom it could rely for protection. The army's self-propelled artillery is close to the end of its usefulness, and some of the army's mortars, jeeps, and trucks, never all that capable, have ended their utility. Wretched twenty-year-old Iltis jeeps were deployed to Afghanistan in 2003, where they broke down continually and, because they were unarmoured, proved vulnerable to land mines.

The main equipment problem the army faces is a shortage of spare parts for its vehicles and weapons systems. Budgetary problems have forced the army to cut back purchases for almost a decade. Now, as Colonel Howie Marsh wrote, "like a destitute family" that kept on "deferring day-to-day maintenance, failed to replace used items and ignored long-term investment," the army is facing collapse. According to the estimates, within the next two or three years perhaps half of the land force's weapons systems and vehicles might be inoperable for periods of up to five years.

In Colonel MacDonald's view, unless major equipment purchases are begun now, the Canadian Forces faces a "mass extinction scenario" beginning in 2010. Rust-out, he argues, will eliminate capabilities one after another—ships, aircraft, artillery, and trucks—until the forces will be reduced to the constabulary that Defence Minister David Collenette assured Canadians in 1994 was not the future of their military.

Canadians do not usually pay much attention to their armed forces except in wartime or when, as during the Somalia affair, the front pages are regularly filled with embarrassing stories. The Canadian Forces worked after Somalia to restore public confidence and, though there were hiccups along the way, the military largely succeeded. The drumbeat of criticism now came from pro-defence critics such as the House of Commons Standing Committee on National Defence and Veterans Affairs and the Senate's National Security Committee, the Conference of Defence Associations, the Council for Canadian Security in the 21st Century, and the Canadian Institute of Strategic Studies.

188

By 2002 and 2003 the continuing trickle of reports on the sorry state of the Canadian Forces had begun to make an impact. The Defence Minister began an online consultation with Canadians in August 2002 that drew an extraordinary 17,642 comments before the site was closed in December. Overwhelmingly, the responses were critical of the state of the forces, their equipment and funding, and the operational tempo to which troops were marching: 79 percent believed that the forces' ability to respond to crises was severely limited because of the lack of long-range transport and ships; 80 percent believed CF strength was too low; 84 percent said the forces did not have the equipment for operations at home and abroad; and 60 percent wanted more investment in high-tech capabilities. Realistically, 87.6 percent maintained that the Defence budget had to be increased to pay for better equipment and more personnel.

That particular opinion sounding, though self-selective and more focused than the usual public opinion surveys, obtained similar results to those published by polling companies. Environics found in June-July 2002 that almost three-quarters of Canadians believed the Canadian Forces lacked the personnel and equipment for operations at home and abroad. Compas reported in July 2002 that 72 percent wanted the defence budget increased. Canadians generally knew and seemed to understand the pathetic state of their Canadian Forces.

The Minister's consultation and the opinion polling took place in the aftermath of the terrorist attacks on New York City and Washington on September 11, 2001, and the beginning of the War on Terrorism. The changed global atmosphere and the increased pressures from George W. Bush for his friends to assist in the war posed a test for Chrétien's administration. The Canadian government failed to rise to the challenge.

First, virtually every observer anticipated that the September 11 attacks would force the federal government to augment defence spending. This increase did not happen until the February 2003 budget, and the sums involved were wholly insufficient to repair decades of damage.

Second, everyone expected that Canada-US defence co-operation would be ramped up. North America itself was under attack. The government did increase its inadequate domestic anti-terrorist measures and eventually banned some, but not all, of the most notorious terrorist organizations that had been permitted to flourish and fundraise in Canada. It stepped up its screening of refugee claimants and immigrants and improved airport security. The huge, new US Department of Homeland Security had no counterpart in the federal bureaucracy, but both countries cooperated in securing their common border. The resulting measures allowed that essential flow of trade goods to continue un-impeded over the increasingly "smart" Canada-US border.

Defence cooperation, however, was less successful. The Chrétien government before September 11 had become expert at irritating the Americans. Its support for a global Anti-Personnel Land Mines Convention was one such example.

The US military, and many Canadian soldiers too, considered land mines a necessary defensive tool, but Canadian Foreign Minister Lloyd Axworthy, using "pulpit diplomacy" to press his "soft power" and "human security" agendas, succeeded in getting the convention through.* The Department of National Defence tried to resist Axworthy's proposal, arguing that its soldiers had always used anti-personnel mines properly, but tamely acquiesced when it failed to win support in the Cabinet. Canada and 121 other nations signed the convention in Ottawa in December 1997; the United States, highly displeased at a treaty it believed limited its ability to protect its troops abroad, did not. Military historian Dean Oliver wrote that land mines had been viewed "as simply a humanitarian problem shorn of military considerations" and that support for the convention "demonstrated the extent to which human security had become firmly entrenched as a distinguishing feature of Canadian security policy." The Department of Foreign Affairs held that Canada needed "peace police," not soldiers.

After September 11, Washington's unhappiness with Ottawa mounted. The US military created Northern

---

*Axworthy's soft-power campaign took place at the same time that UN operations expanded exponentially and grew more dangerous. At its peak in the mid-1990s, Canada had 5,000 troops on peace operations, in low-, mid-, and high-intensity conflicts. The *Washington Post* on February 20, 1999, characterized Axworthy as "a moralizing foreign minister from a middle-power country" with a "touchy-feely approach."

Command in October 2002, with responsibilities covering all North America. The Ottawa response was minimal, as Canada, amid widespread and inflammatory anti-American outbursts, did nothing more than dispatch a small planning cell to work with the new US command at its Colorado Springs headquarters. Washington then stepped up pressure for a Ballistic Missile Defense System, designed to stop accidental missile strikes from China or Russia or potential attacks by "rogue states" such as Iran and North Korea. Canada's role had to be decided. Now heading a research centre in Vancouver, Axworthy again led the charge against participation in this defence system, as did Liberal leadership candidate Sheila Copps, but in the spring of 2003 the government decided to begin discussions with the United States on Canadian participation. Canada had already waited too long, for the Pentagon had determined the system's architecture and chosen its sites, though the intercept system had not yet been made to function effectively. The Canadian goal, quite properly, was to put the Ballistic Missile Defense System under the North American Air Defence Command, where Canada was a full partner. If NORAD was not the reporting headquarters for the missile system, then that alliance, almost a half-century old, could be vitiated and, with it, such influence Canada has on the US military's planning for continental defence. But why would the United States agree, after watching anti-Americanism run wild in

Canada after September 11 and observing the Chrétien government's attitude during the Iraq War?

Ottawa was markedly unhelpful to the United States as it tried to move through the United Nations Security Council to muster support for an attack on Saddam Hussein. The Americans' stated aim was to eliminate Iraq's weapons of mass destruction—biological and chemical weapons and a nuclear weapons research program. Sufficient cause for action, in my view, was that Saddam Hussein was a brutal dictator, a monster who had attacked Iran and Kuwait and oppressed his own people. The Canadian approach at the United Nations was to find a "compromise," to delay, to stall. The government's ultimate position was that Canada would not support the United States and its one solid ally, Tony Blair's Great Britain, unless the UN Security Council gave its authorization. But France and Germany paralyzed the council's work, and the US-led coalition invaded Iraq and seized Baghdad in the spring of 2003.

Canada refused to participate militarily or to offer political support, though the decision was finally determined not by Ottawa but by the Security Council's inaction in New York. The Quebec provincial election was under way at the time, and all three party leaders sported anti-war ribbons in the single televised leaders' debate. Such solidarity no doubt encouraged Chrétien in his Iraq policy. When the provincial Liberals defeated the separatist Parti Québécois, the Prime

Minister must have believed that his Iraq policy had contributed to the result. So did others. Alberta Senator-elect Ted Morton bluntly noted: "As the Iraqi war reminded us, Canadian foreign policy is set by public opinion in Quebec, which has meant abandoning our historical allies."

There appeared to be some truth in Morton's comment. Polling for Global TV, JM-CK Communications tested opinion on the coming war in March 2003 and found that 77.6 percent of Quebeckers had unfavourable views of the US government (compared with 54.8 percent favourable views in the rest of the nation), and that the overall attitude was "Don't participate. The majority of Quebeckers support not doing anything at all" about Iraq. Quebec opinion did not change. In April the difference between Quebec (29 percent supporting the war) and Alberta (62 percent supporting) was huge. Other provinces were less supportive than Alberta, but supportive nonetheless. Not since conscription during the Second World War had the split in opinion between francophone Quebec and English Canada been so great.

For its part, shortly before the Americans abandoned their efforts at United Nations headquarters, the Chrétien government decided to deploy troops to Afghanistan, thereby guaranteeing that Canada could do nothing militarily in Iraq. Acceptance of this mission stunned senior officers at National Defence Headquarters, and one major-general resigned in protest. It did not seem to matter that Canada's land forces were already grossly overextended and burnt out, or that troops would be in danger from warlords' armies and land mines and subject to attack from Taliban remnants in volatile Kabul. Even though the Canadian Forces had lost capability between 1999 and 2003, the Prime Minister confirmed his self-image as a peacemaker by offering to dispatch Canadian troops simultaneously to the civil war in the Democratic Republic of the Congo and to the terrorist-infested border between Israel and the nascent Palestinian state. The Canadian Forces had no troops available, and almost no means to transport or support troops even if they could be found, but these facts did not concern Chrétien. Soldiers were tools of government to be used as the Prime Minister directed.* Ottawa pandered to the public's increasingly virulent anti-Americanism, and happily, stupidly, refused George W. Bush.

The root of the problem was how best to defend Canadian sovereignty. The United States was a superpower with vast and growing global responsibilities and, after September 11,

---

*In February 2000 the Chief of the Defence Staff explained to a small group that his job was to tell the government of the impact of operations on troops and equipment. Then the government has to decide. If thousands are dying, the Canadian Forces has to go; if it is a major domestic crisis, the Canadian Forces must participate. But it is the government that decides. "I am not the conscience of my country," the CDS said. "I make recommendations and the government decides."

a wholly justifiable concern about homeland security and defence. It was one thing for Ottawa to hang back on foreign expeditions, though al-Qaeda and the Saddam Husseins of the world threaten Canada as much as they do the United States and Britain.* But it was another matter entirely to go slow on North American defence, to delay negotiations with the United States on Ballistic Missile Defense, and to refuse to increase the Canadian Forces' ability to defend Canadian soil. The coming collapse of the air force's Aurora surveillance aircraft, for example, did not send a comforting message to Washington. Neither did tying up the navy at the docks at Halifax and Esquimalt.

In these circumstances, who should be surprised if the United States takes the steps it believes are necessary in its own defence—and then tells Ottawa after the fact? How will such an event advance Canadian sovereignty? Despite his forty years in Parliament and his almost eleven years as Prime Minister, Jean Chrétien never learned that, by cooperating with the superpower neighbour, by getting a seat at the table where the decisions are made, Canada could actually enhance its sovereignty. This standing requires a willingness

---

*As a result of the Canadian position on the Iraq War, Canada is now excluded from the "tight intelligence circle that it developed with Washington, London and Canberra," according to journalist Matthew Fisher in the *National Post*, August 8, 2003. If so, this exclusion is very damaging to the protection of Canada's national interests.

to pay the costs of a proper defence force, and this adequate defence is, in turn, a measure of sovereignty. Instead, what Chrétien offered was rhetorical sovereignty, the illusion of independence, and the turning over of North American defence to the United States. Even more alarming, Ottawa pretended to itself and to its citizens that this transfer had not happened.

Chrétien's Liberal regime had handled defence questions shamefully in its nearly eleven years in power, and virtually all the unhappy trends of the last half-century came to their apogee during his time in office. He failed to fund the Canadian Forces adequately, ran down its strength, and allowed major weapons systems to fall into obsolescence, often at risk to the soldiers, sailors, and aircrew who operated them. He let down Canada's major ally and practised anti-Americanism as policy in ways that had not been seen since John Diefenbaker held power four decades ago. He and his ministers pandered to neutralist sentiments, not least in Quebec. He continued to lust after kudos at the United Nations, and his government used Canada's fighting personnel to the point of exhaustion.

In a book on Pierre Trudeau's foreign policy published in 1990, Robert Bothwell and I described the years from 1968 to 1984 as "a long, dark night of the spirit" for the military. That darkness lasted beyond 1984 through the Mulroney and Chrétien years and it continues still, its gloom increasing daily. At the end of 2003 the Canadian Forces' personnel were exhausted, their equipment rusted out, their coffers all but empty. The Chrétien government, without question, has been the worst since the Second World War in its shameful treatment of the country's military: worse than Diefenbaker's in so neglecting threats to North America's security that it infuriated the United States; worse than Trudeau's in allowing the rust-out of the Canadian Forces' equipment and in pandering to quasi-neutralist sentiment; worse even than Mulroney's in offering a White Paper and instantly trashing it. Who finished off the Canadian Forces? There can be no doubt about my answer: Jean Chrétien did.

CHAPTER 7

The Way Ahead:
Resurrecting
the Canadian Military

So, who killed the Canadian military? Our politicians must take the major share of the credit for dismantling Canada's armed forces over the last forty years. In truth, it made little difference who was in power. The Liberals and Conservatives never cared much for the armed forces, although at times they pretended interest, and the New Democrats were always unredeemably hostile to military spending. Nor did it make much difference whether the Prime Minister was French- or English-speaking. The military was low on the priority list for all.

Some of our generals also did their part in killing the Canadian Forces through bad judgment. Some were incompetent, venal trimmers who rose through low cunning more than high military skills. These men did not make up the great majority of our senior commanders, however. Nor were junior officers and non-commissioned members of the Canadian Forces all as brutal or corrupt as the media sometimes painted them. Ninety-nine of every hundred were in the forces because they loved the comradeship and believed they were serving their country. Some of the killers of the military wore uniforms, to be sure, but even they do not deserve all the blame that the press and their political masters have at times placed on them. The politicians were far more important in destroying the Canadian Forces, and they had very effective allies in the voters of Canada.

At root, the real killers of the Canadian Forces were you and I, the Canadian people. The military scarcely interested us, and we paid it no attention. We assumed that we were safe, our territory inviolable, and we believed ultimately that the Americans would protect us. So you and I elected our politicians, and we told them in opinion polls that we wanted health care, culture, better pensions, and a thousand other programs from the government. These were all good things, and we need them. But Canada is a rich country, and we could have had both a strong military *and* the social services we want. Who killed the Canadian military? Ultimately, the Canadian people did.

By our indifference to the Canadian Forces, by our unwillingness to demand that troops dispatched overseas have everything they need to protect themselves and to operate effectively, Canadians colluded with governments that sought cheap popularity by being a chore boy for the United Nations and refusing to cooperate fully with our friends. The media focused on petty military scandals rather than the gross scandal of governments failing to equip, sustain, and train our service personnel properly. As a result, we

Canadians failed to demand that soldiers, sailors, and air-crew got the modern equipment they needed—to fight and win, to train realistically, to operate effectively on their own, and to cooperate with our allies.

One of this nation's great strengths is that Canadians care and that they want to do good. They want to participate in UN operations if lives can be saved by intervention. An Ipsos-Reid opinion poll in February 1994 found that an extraordinary three out of four Canadians supported UN peacekeeping. A similar question two-and-a-half years later observed that 55 percent were in favour of Canada continuing to take a leading role in peacekeeping—a striking number, considering that the scandals arising out of the Canadian Airborne Regiment's actions in Somalia had come to light. Canadians loved peacekeeping, and Quebec, traditionally the most anti-military region of the country, seemed to be much the same as English-speaking Canada in its attitude.

For all their support of peacekeeping, however, Canadians seem to know little about it. An Ipsos-Reid poll conducted for the Dominion Institute and released on Canada Day, 2003, asked Canadians for the name of the "new type of U.N.-mandated force" created by Lester Pearson during the 1956 Suez Crisis. Only 44 percent could produce the answer "peacekeepers": only 32 percent in Quebec responded correctly, and in Saskatchewan and Manitoba, the highest scoring region, just 50 percent did so.

203

In the same Ipsos-Reid/Dominion Institute study, Canadians were asked to name two international peace-keeping missions in which Canada had participated since 1990. There had been missions in the former Yugoslavia, Somalia, Rwanda, Haiti, the Congo, Ethiopia, Angola, Sierra Leone, the Central African Republic, Guatemala, Mozambique, Namibia, East Timor, and more, but only 41 percent of Canadians could name two operations in which the Canadian Forces had served. The lowest correct response rate was in Atlantic Canada (32 percent); the best in British Columbia and Alberta (47 percent). Canadians may talk a great deal about peacekeeping, but only in the most general and uninformed of ways. We talk a good game, in other words.

That point is important, I think, because Canadians do not appear to comprehend that a military exists to fight wars and, ultimately, to protect the national interests. Instead, they somehow came to think of the Canadian Forces as the embodiment of their values, as peacekeeping social workers at home and abroad. By letting our governments put women into combat units and lowering training standards to accommodate them, by accepting the idea of quotas for visible minorities in the military, Canadians let their values run ahead of their reason. The kinder, gentler peace machine, the "not Americans"—that was our Canadian Forces. Canadians and their successive governments, both Liberal and

Conservative, have turned the Canadian Forces into a bad joke that will take a decade and tens of billions of dollars to set right. Who killed the Canadian military? We all did.

Where do we go from here? How do we fix what is broken and preserve what works? What should we do and how much will it cost?

Canadians must decide—for the first time in our history—what their national interests really are. If we know that, we can begin to consider how best to protect and advance them. I believe these interests should be as follows:

- Canada must safeguard its territory and the security of its people, and work to maintain its national unity.
- Canada must act to maintain and enhance its independence.
- Canada must promote the nation's economic growth to enhance its prosperity.
- Canada must work with its friends for democracy and freedom.

Every nation has to defend its own territory and people and remain as independent as possible in a shrinking and increasingly interconnected world. Every nation must try to improve its people's lot. And, since nations need allies and our history tells us we can be threatened by dictatorships and theocracies, this nation must work with its friends to minimize short- and long-term threats to us.

The difficulties come when we try to prioritize these interests. Maintaining national unity has always been difficult for Canada because French and English Canadians have different perceptions of the world. It is no easy task when politicians discover, as Mackenzie King did in 1939 or Jean Chrétien in 2003, that Quebec attitudes to participation in war are both strikingly more pacifistic (and in 2003 more anti-American) than those in English Canada generally or, in 2003, in Alberta most particularly. Skilful politicians must find the balance on questions of peace and war, and this, historically, has been the test of great leadership. King took us into war on terms that won him the acquiescence of Quebec, but Chrétien refused to participate in the Iraq War in a manner that left many English-speaking Canadians outraged. Who served unity best? Which course best protected Canada's interests?

At the same time, Canada has to promote its economic growth. More than 40 percent of our gross domestic product and some 30 percent of our jobs come from trade with the United States, and almost 85 percent of our exports go to or pass through the United States. Thus, our leaders have to be very aware of the importance of keeping the southbound trade channels open. We have seen the hurt inflicted on the beef industry by a single case of mad cow disease or on our wood products industries by disputes over softwood lumber. In fact, the vast majority of Canadian products enter the United States without difficulty, and our prosperity and our jobs depend on this trade. The United States is a superpower, and Canada is not. Very simply, our leaders must cut their cloth to fit our situation. We cannot offend the United States too often or too grievously or we will pay a serious price. Canada can be brought to its knees not by a US invasion or a dramatic closing of the border but by a few moments of extra inspection time by US Customs and Immigration officers at the border. The passengers at Pearson, Trudeau, and Vancouver international airports and the trucks at Fort Erie and Windsor will be backed up for kilometres. Given the security fears in the United States, given Canada's sometimes lax efforts at tracking down terrorists, the Americans will believe themselves justified in acting toughly. Keeping the Yanks happy, or at least not angry, must be a national interest.

Canadians, historically, have seen the fourth national interest—helping our friends—as important. Most continue to do so today. Canadians want to be good international citizens. They support our participation in United Nations peacekeeping and peacemaking efforts, as the opinion polls make clear, and they support Canada sending troops, ships, and aircraft to the War on Terrorism. Where we get into arguments is when the United States is taking the lead, because Canadian anti-Americanism still remains powerful, President George W. Bush is hugely unpopular in Canada, and Canadians always fear that their independence might be lost or diminished by, God forbid, agreeing with the Yanks or following their lead too closely. Like our need to maintain unity, our need to keep trade flowing, this anti-Americanism is a political problem of major proportions, and the skill with which leaders manage this question determines their failure or success.

One other factor should be stated clearly. The United States is not going to disappear. Canada is joined to the United States and will remain so. Geography has made us neighbours, and by and large we are extremely lucky in having the Americans next door. We might have been Poland, sandwiched between the Germans and the Russians. Unlike us, the Americans take their national defence seriously, and never more so than after September 11, 2001. They have long had concern for their northern frontier, and since Franklin Roosevelt's day they have worried that Canada wasn't doing enough to keep its territory protected. During the Second World War, Canada began to pay attention to these concerns, and after the war we and the Americans built radar lines in the north and combined our air defence commands into NORAD, sensibly maximizing resources and giving Canadians some genuine say in the decisions on continental defence. The questions today involve Ballistic Missile

Defense, coastal security, and tighter immigration, refugee, and border screening controls, but the basic issue has not changed. Canada has to act so that no threat to the United States will ever be facilitated by Canadian weakness. We must also ensure that the Americans do not believe we are getting a free ride on their heavily laden backs. Neutrality is not an option for Canada because the Americans cannot permit it. Since the United States will always be there, each generation, each Canadian government, needs to come to grips with this reality.

Doing so is not pandering to the United States; rather, it's in our own interest. The threats to the United States were, and are, threats to Canada too. If the Cold War had turned hot, Montreal, Toronto, and Vancouver would have been incinerated, along with New York, Chicago, and Los Angeles. If terrorists were unable to strike at US territory, they might attack the US Embassy in Ottawa or huge cruise ships full of American tourists tied up at the piers in Halifax or Vancouver. They might attack wholly Canadian targets too, because we are everything the Islamic terrorists hate—a democratic, secular, pluralist society. Only the naïve (a group that appears to include far too many federal ministers and politicians) could believe otherwise. Geography has made us neighbours, but history has put us in the same boat, and, ultimately, we will sink or swim with the Americans. Even Margaret Atwood, a true-believing nationalist always deeply sceptical of the

Americans, said, "We know perfectly well that if [the US] goes down the plug-hole, we're going with [it]."

But how can we preserve our sovereign independence if we're at sea in that boat with the Yanks? That is the real test. Some Canadians believe the way to proceed is to kick the Americans at every opportunity, disagreeing with Washington just to demonstrate our independence, damning their leaders as bastards, and opposing their policies as imperialistic and militaristic. Some think the best defence for Canada is to turn its back on Washington.

In a talk I gave at McGill University in late 2002, a student said to applause that he'd rather Canada had no military at all; how else could we stop the United States from using the Canadian Forces to serve American interests? I replied that his view was an abjectly colonial response. Taking a free ride is cheap today but dear tomorrow. The only way Canada can get any share in making the decisions that will affect us for decades to come is to be present when those decisions are made. We have a say in continental air defence because we belong to NORAD and have a few military assets to deploy. If we have no military, someone in Washington will decide on policy without consulting Ottawa, and those decisions will of course include the defence of continental North America, including Canada. For us, that will be the antithesis of sovereignty. That will be colonialism.

Colonies have no say in Great Power decisions. We ought

to know that from our history. Canada went into the First World War in August 1914 because Britain did; the United Kingdom declaration of war bound Canada. In September 1939 we were theoretically independent but still psychologically colonial; we made our own declaration of war seven days after Britain's, and if Britain had decided not to fight on September 3, we too would have remained neutral. Participation gets you the right to a share in decisions, and that, in an interdependent world, is the only realistic definition of sovereignty for a small power. Turning your back lets others make the decisions and, if you are unhappy with them, tough. You pay a political and psychic price for colonialism. I would rather be a realist.

No Canadian should ever believe that American national interests are ours. Certainly I don't. Our interests are similar, our values are closer to each other's than we want to admit, and we are friends. Nonetheless, the United States thinks and acts globally, and we only pretend to do so; the United States has unrivalled power, and we are a pygmy. The Americans are tough in advancing their interests. We curse the damn Yankees and rely on brainpower to let us hold our own— and, by doing so, we have survived and prospered for many decades. Still, the Americans are neighbours, and they are shrewd enough to know that they benefit from telling the world that they enjoy having an independent nation to their north. As they do.

But the Americans are fierce in protecting their national security interests. Their actions will create enemies who will automatically threaten us because of where we are located and the values we profess. There is not much we can do about it other than be prepared. The ways in which the Americans organize both their military forces and the attitudes they take to the world will also affect us in major ways. It's essential, then, that we know what our national interests are and think clearly about how to advance them. I am convinced we will do better if we work with the United States, when we can, than if we challenge and defy the Americans out of "little brother" hubris. Chrétien once said unguardedly, "I make it my policy" not to do what the United States wants. "It's popular." It is popular, unfortunately, but it's also just plain stupid. Nor does it serve our real national interests.

We can oppose US foreign or trade policy if we choose to do so, but good sense suggests we must pick our spots carefully and understand in advance that there may be a price to pay. We should also recognize that working quietly behind the scenes is better than having ministers and MPs slander the President and all his works in public. Cheap nationalist diatribes pander to the worst among us. Getting on with the neighbours requires a major effort, both for homeowners and for nations, and it will always be in the Canadian interest to make that effort to be on the best possible terms with the United States.

Paul Martin, our new Prime Minister, appears to understand the realities of the situation and the proper way to protect Canadian sovereignty. In an interview with the *National Post*, published on April 29, 2003, he said, "I'm just not worried about the United States invading us. I just don't want the Americans to think that they've got to come up and protect themselves by protecting us. The definition of sovereignty is we will assure our partners in North America that we can protect the northern half of North America." He continued that such defence required "further military spending" and pointed especially to better intelligence gathering, "military personnel and also equipment—no doubt about that." Martin now has the opportunity to fulfill his promises.*

How do we interpret our interests and the realities we live with? What kind of defence policies do we need? What kind of Canadian Forces will we require to protect us in a new and frightening world of terrorism?

213

---

*On August 8, 2003, Martin declined to respond to a question from the *National Post*, asked of party leaders, on "what immediate changes you would make to Canada's defence policy." What his views and actions in office will be remain unclear.

No one suggests that Canada once more raise the 630,000-man army we produced in the Great War or the 1.1 million men and women we put into uniform in the Second World War. No matter how much some of us might wish it, no one even suggests that we have the 120,000 professional soldiers, sailors, and aircrew we kept in uniform at the peak of the Cold War. We don't truly need such numbers today (though it will always be sensible to have mobilization plans to create a large force filed away). We need enough of a military to do three things:

- To defend Canada and, in cooperation with the United States, the whole of North America.
- To provide the "last-resort" force to protect domestic order and to assist in disasters.
- To work with our friends in coalition and alliance forces and to join in UN and other international efforts to keep and enforce the peace.

These defence priorities have been, in one form or another, those we have followed since we joined NATO in 1949. Nothing has changed to make them less important today. If Paul Martin sets up, as he should, a defence review (at the same time as, or jointly with, a foreign policy review), these priorities will almost certainly be maintained. A serious review of where we are and where we want to go is a pre-condition for real renewal of the Canadian Forces; it is also a test of political leadership for the new Prime Minister. We must have, as John Ferris of the University of Calgary put it, a "defence policy [that] fits a 9/10 world." The new Prime Minister has to make our military policy actually work in a post–September 11 world.

To meet these priorities, we need a National Defence Headquarters that can function well, plan effectively, and produce agreed strategic concepts which recognize that the three services must work together. We require a navy, an air force, and an army equipped with modern weaponry, and we need reservists to back up all three services. We need bases located across the country. We need to train our service-men and women to fight wars in the sure confidence that, if they can fight well, they can also handle the full range of peace operations. We require the capacity to get well-trained troops and their gear to critical points in Canada or overseas quickly. We need defence industries that can supply the services with everything from bullets to frigates, and that can only be secured if we can give real guarantees of funding for at least five to ten years ahead; otherwise, we must acquire almost all defence equipment abroad. We should not, however, tie procurement to a tyrannical policy of industrial offsets aimed at creating jobs in economically

215

starved regions. Value for money, only slightly modified to accommodate other national goals, must be our watchword.*

All these ideas cost money and require trained personnel, and it is the task of government to provide both. We also need a government that does not overcommit its military, that is careful to weigh the benefits of participation against both Canada's interests and the military's capabilities. A government with good sense, in other words.

Let me outline my ideas for what the Canadian Forces needs in the opening years of the twenty-first century.

First, National Defence Headquarters needs to be reformed. The combined civilian-military staff has produced only the civilianization and politicization of the military, and neither is tolerable. But it is difficult to push Humpty Dumpty off the wall without creating a mess on the ground,

---

*A perfect example of how not to do it was the contract for the wretched Iltis patrol vehicle, let in 1982. The Iltis was German-designed and could be purchased there for $26,500 each. But Ottawa decided to help out Bombardier and gave it the contract—at $84,000 for each vehicle. If the offsets had added, say, $10,000 to the cost of each vehicle, that might have been acceptable. To increase costs by almost $60,000, however, was scandalous. Even worse, field trials of the Iltis before the order was placed found much fault with the design, but these complaints were blamed on the inexperience of the soldiers testing the vehicle. Only in Canada, you say? Pity.

and great care must be taken to avoid chaos. Any defence review should include a subcommittee charged with assessing how best to recreate a Canadian Forces Headquarters that can work with the Deputy Minister's staff in running the Department of National Defence and the Canadian Forces.

The navy requires a fleet to patrol Canada's territorial limits against threats ranging from weapons of mass destruction to immigrant smugglers and also to work with our friends in NATO and in coalitions of the willing. To do this dual role properly will require a 50-percent increase of its manpower strength to some 12,000, so that the sea-going personnel can be raised to 6,500 and tied-up ships can be brought back into service. That will allow for more regular rotations through sea duty without overstraining the fleet's personnel. The naval reserve should be increased by 50 percent to some 6,000, enough to provide crews for the Maritime Coastal Defence Vessels (MCDVs) and to undertake the reserve's other chores—including homeland defence in the cities in which the naval reserve operates.

The navy requires the replacement of its four rusted-out and obsolete destroyers and the expeditious refitting of its capable frigates. There is need for three or four multipurpose amphibious transports (JSS, or Joint Support Ships, in current NDHQ jargon) to replace the two over-age AORs or replenishment ships. With new support ships, Canada will be able to supply its fleet on operations abroad and get troops

217

and their equipment overseas quickly, without having to hunt for a Liberian- or Panamanian-registered freighter to charter. And the government must place and maintain naval orders on a long-term basis so our shipyards can produce at least one major naval vessel a year, sustaining the fleet and preserving invaluable industrial skills. We know we will need new ships as the frigates and coastal defence vessels wear out, so why not phase in their construction and commissioning? If these orders create (or restore) highly skilled trades in Saint John, New Brunswick, and Lévis, Quebec, and if the domestic costs are roughly comparable to what we would pay offshore, that is an intended bonus.

The navy also needs to strengthen its already well-developed links with the US Navy.

Inter-operability is invaluable,* and Canada should continue the five-year-long practice of attaching a frigate to a US Navy carrier battle group. That gives the navy access to US intelligence and reconnaissance networks denied to virtually all other nations. At the same time, the navy should further develop its own task-group concept. A Canadian navy task group consists of one to three frigates, a destroyer as the command ship, and a replenishment vessel, all operating as a

---

*The navy's 2001 strategy document, *Leadmark*, correctly makes the point that inter-operability does not weaken Canadian sovereignty. "Rather, because each mission is a function of choice, it tends to strengthen Canadian sovereignty."

unit. The task group allows the Canadian navy to operate independently of other navies if it chooses, and it is a "force multiplier" for each of the individual ships. It creates a distinctively Canadian identity at sea when that is necessary or otherwise desirable. It has also given Canadian commanders a lead position in multinational deployments, as recently demonstrated in the War on Terrorism.

The navy leadership deserves high marks for the way it has run its reserves and, indeed, all its ships. The reservists have a role—primarily to crew the coastal defence vessels—and they do it well. Appointing prominent Canadians as Honorary Naval Captains also helps in the fight for public opinion. Historically weak in francophone Quebec, the navy responded by putting its reserve headquarters in Quebec City, a clever move. And by naming its ships after cities big and small (Kingston-class MCDVs, Victoria-class submarines, and Halifax-class frigates), the navy creates instant and enthusiastic public support. I attended a dinner in Calgary where the captain of HMCS *Calgary* was treated like an old friend, the bearer of the city's name, best wishes, and support. Neither the army nor the air force has shown comparable ingenuity and good sense.

The army will likely continue to bear the burden of supporting Canadian commitments abroad. It cannot do so with its present strength of 20,000 overworked and stressed-out men and women and requires another 10,000 soldiers. That will be sufficient to bring the units of the present three brigade groups up to their establishment strength of 6,000 (from around 4,000 today), to allow for an expansion of the JTF-2 special forces unit to, say, 900 all ranks, and to relieve the pressure on the training system, presently buckling under the strain of deployments abroad. How to organize the brigades is open to discussion: either one medium-weight mechanized brigade and two light brigades, or three brigade groups each with two completely mechanized battalions and one light infantry battalion—like the 3rd Battalion of the Princess Patricia's Canadian Light Infantry which did so well in Afghanistan in 2002. Both variants can work.

What is key is that the army's strategic thinking is now well developed. The generals understand the importance of being able to process information quickly on the battlefield and delivering precision munitions on target. They know they must emphasize close operations in complex terrain, operations in places as various as urban Kabul or the deserts and mountains of Afghanistan. The battlefield, said the former Chief of the Land Staff, Lieutenant-General Mike Jeffrey, "is going to become more diverse and there is a role for us in a combat role on that diverse battlefield." General Jeffrey understood that soldiers trained for that diverse battlefield could fulfill every task asked of them, ranging from firefighting in British Columbia to peace enforcement in Bosnia and war in Afghanistan.

To fight successfully on this diverse terrain, the army needs a direct fire-support capability, either a new main battle tank or an armoured vehicle like the eight-wheeled American Stryker, mobile and equipped with a 105-mm gun. Heavy armour proved itself again in Iraq in 2003, so tanks would be preferable, not least because they can defend themselves better against rocket-propelled grenades, the irregulars' weapon of choice. The lightly armoured Stryker, which the United States is trying out in Iraq beginning in late 2003, is surprisingly heavy and difficult to transport even in the newest model of Hercules C-130Js. While Strykers would be useful, in my view, they are not tanks and cannot be employed as if they were. I believe the army should have two tank regiments. The Germans have reportedly offered Canada a variant of Leopard II tanks at a bargain-basement price, likely less than the cost of Strykers. We ought to take them up on their offer, but even if we do not, we must continue to think about armoured warfare. It *will* not disappear, even if we have no tanks.

The army also needs new medium-support vehicles, replacements for its mortars and light artillery, a new direct-fire weapon, improved anti-tank capability, and continued improvements to its information systems. It requires more Combat Service Support—logistics units, in other words—so it does not need to rely on potentially unreliable civilian contractors on unpredictable overseas operations.

The army's object should be to produce a medium-weight force with punch, but one that can also send infantry up hills and operate as armoured cavalry and in reconnaissance roles with a coalition force. "Transformation" is today's fashionable military buzzword, and it means breaking away from the heavyweight fighting posture of the Cold War to a lighter, much more mobile, logistically self-sufficient force. This flexibility should be the army's goal. It will be a mistake if the government and National Defence Headquarters fixate on one or two niches that glimmer like purest ore today and turn into fool's gold tomorrow. Some Canadians will surely tell the new Prime Minister's defence review in 2004 that UN peacekeeping—or mine-clearing or mountain troops or civil affairs units to operate in occupied territory—ought to be the Canadian niche, but they will all be completely wrong. Every war that comes along requires a new mix of units. In Iraq in 1991 it was heavy armour; in Afghanistan in 2003 it was light infantry; and in Iraq in 2003 it was fast armour followed by civil affairs and military police. Multipurpose and combat capable—those are the key principles that the Canadian government and the Canadian Forces must follow.

222

Whatever course we choose, the army must be able to dispatch a battle group abroad on short order—on Canadian aircraft and Canadian navy ships, not charters secured on the open market—and follow it up with the rest of a fully equipped brigade within sixty to ninety days. It must be able to sustain this force, providing reinforcements to replace casualties. We cannot achieve these modest goals today. To do so in the near future, the army needs more soldiers. It needs regular, annual training exercises on a brigade—or larger—scale, and it must train its soldiers for war-fighting. It is worth repeating this maxim: a well-trained soldier can deal with everything from blue beret observer duties through tense blue helmet confrontations, up to and including a major war. Well-disciplined, skilled in the use of all weapons, the trained soldier is useful in many different contingencies. A soldier trained only for peacekeeping duties—a member of a gendarmerie, in other words—can handle only low-end peacekeeping and cannot step up to war-fighting without extensive retraining and re-equipping. The utility of a gendarmerie is strictly limited. For a small nation with limited budgets and a tiny military, it makes no sense to have a uni-dimensional military, given the wide spectrum of possible threats we face.

The army, moreover, must be able to respond to domestic crises, ranging from floods to earthquakes and including terrorist attacks using weapons of mass destruction. It needs to bring the contingents home from Bosnia and Afghanistan as soon as possible, and Canada ought not to accept any new commitments for at least the next two years. The army needs a militia of some 25,000, based in communities across the land and trained and well equipped for homeland defence (which means trained to deal with nuclear, chemical, and bacteriological attacks), for mobilization tasks, and for supplying trained fill-in personnel for regular force deployments (eighty reservists were included in the first rotation of the army's Afghanistan deployment in 2003–4, for example). And militia units for the first time are now beginning to form direct working links with police and fire departments, a sensible response to the terrorist threat. For a hard-pressed police force in, say, Toronto, a militia that could put 2,000 to 3,000 trained men and women on the streets in an emergency could be of enormous assistance. The Canadian Forces' Disaster Assistance Response Team, intended to assist with humanitarian disasters, is another unit of great utility for tasks in homeland defence and an aid to the civil authority.

The air force requires another 5,000 personnel in its regular force and an expansion of its reserve force. It needs to speed up the refitting of its CF-18s and should keep a close watch on—and a financial stake in—the international development of the Joint Strike Fighter. We may want a new fighter aircraft in the coming decade. What the air force needs desperately is a new helicopter to replace the Sea King. Without it, the utility of the navy's destroyers and frigates is greatly limited. (Paul Martin said that if Chrétien did not replace the Sea Kings, he would "resolve [this question] quickly.") The air force needs more (and more upgraded) maritime patrol aircraft to protect Canadian sovereignty in the North and at sea. Some of these aircraft served in the War on Terrorism, so their capabilities can also help to meet Canadian obligations abroad. The lifespan of the Auroras used in this role will expire in 2009, and planning for a replacement ought to be in hand now.

The air force urgently needs new medium-range transport aircraft to replace the ancient Hercules fleet before planes and their crews begin to fall out of the sky. And the air force requires a squadron of four to six C-17s, huge, long-range transports, for both domestic and overseas purposes. (A cheaper alternative might be to buy some of the large C-5 transports the US Air Force is taking out of service.) If the need arose to send troops and equipment to Quebec for another great ice storm or to British Columbia to help fight forest fires or do rescue work after an earthquake, Canada ought to be able to transport what is needed in its own aircraft. After the last ice storm, heavy transports had to be begged from the US Air Force.* If Canada needed to evacuate its troops from Kabul, heavy lift aircraft would be invaluable. It is madness to rely, as we now do, on leasing or

---

*In his memoirs of his time as Defence Minister, *Damn the Torpedoes: My Fight to Unify Canada's Armed Forces*, Paul Hellyer talked about the RCAF's unwillingness to spend money on air transport. "They abhorred the idea of being seen as 'truck drivers for the army.' Any airman worth his salt had to be a 'Captain of the Clouds,' an air-superiority, one-on-one type. . . . If the department had any money for airplanes, the RCAF wanted it to be reserved for fighters." Traces of this attitude still linger.

chartering heavy lift from the Ukraine or to plan on sharing c-17s with other NATO nations. Do we really believe that such aircraft will be available in a major international crisis? Prime Minister Chrétien and Defence Minister McCallum seemed to, but they are dead wrong.* Declassified memoranda make clear that the military planners have told the government its ideas are neither cost effective nor militarily sound. Naturally, no politician listened.

The air force reserve also needs revitalization, an identity of its own, and a clearly defined role in homeland defence. Its numbers should be doubled. In the 1990s this reserve brilliantly created a few airfield maintenance units by striking alliances with small town public works departments. It needs similar ingenuity to rebuild itself across Canada.

The additional personnel needed for the three regular force environments comes to just under 20,000. For the purple trades, the Canadian Forces' unified support services, 5,000 more ought to be sufficient to deal with this increase. In other words, the Canadian Forces must be raised towards a strength of 85,000, or more or less where we were at the end of the

---

*Talking to CBC-TV in March 2002, Chrétien said: "Transportation, you know, we have to transport them all the time and we can rent planes. We don't have to have a series of planes on the tarmac to transport them." The transportation of Cabinet ministers was, however, a different matter, and the Prime Minister had no hesitation in using the DND budget to buy executive jets for governmental use.

1980s. The three reserve forces, presently numbering some 22,000, need an additional 20,000 personnel. The requirements for homeland defence, as well as the need to support commitments abroad, demand no less. This is a modest wish list—not five brigade groups, not an airborne brigade, not an aircraft carrier, not new fighter aircraft today, but simply what a small nation must have at its disposal as a bare minimum to meet the needs of the present and of the next decade. The object must be to give Canada a military that, while relatively small, is rapidly deployable, light but lethal, and able to function effectively on the new digital battlefield.

It is also necessary that the navy, army, and air force be able to work and fight together. "Whatever the environment," General Jeffrey said in May 2001, "future operations must be considered as joint . . . conducted by all components from a common perspective"—a unified force, in other words, with all its components working together to serve the nation's interests. If Canada had a senior military leadership that actually believed in this approach, it might be an achievable goal. Unfortunately, we don't as yet.

Canada's forces must also be ready to work jointly with our friends. "If you can't work with your allies," Captain (Navy) Robert Thomas asked, "who do you want to work with?" Inter-operability can only be achieved by training and standardization of weapons and procedures, and inter-operability, while it doesn't require that Canada participate in every coalition operation, allows us to do so when we wish. As a bare minimum, all units charged with continental defence roles—and let's be clear, that is virtually the entire Canadian Forces—*must* be able to work with US forces. That means devoting time and money to training and to upgrading our military information technology capabilities to bring them level with those of our neighbour. Anything less means abandoning the responsibilities and obligations of homeland defence and sovereignty.

Such a force will cost much more than the present $12 billion, or 1.1 percent of GDP, we spend on defence. The extra personnel, regular and reserve, that I suggest will be at least an additional $1.5 billion each year, once the Canadian Forces is increased to its full strength. The equipment needed will cost much more. Naval vessels, destroyers or frigates, now cost close to $1.25 billion each; c-17 long-range transports sell for $400 million apiece; c-130Js, the new Hercules transports, cost $200 million each; and precision guided munitions are very expensive. Armoured vehicles are costly, as well, and so is their regular maintenance. To maintain the army's Coyote reconnaissance vehicles costs $25 million a year, compared with $4.5 million for the vehicle it replaced; new army communications gear will require $60 million a year in upkeep, compared with $8 million at present. New trucks, mortars, and ammunition also cost dearly. And, after years of neglecting infrastructure such as runways, hangars, and docks, allowing the deterioration of permanent married quarters on Canadian Forces bases and delaying environmental clean-ups, huge sums are required for at least a decade to make good the shortfalls of the past. For example, the roof of a building at Valcartier collapsed in 1997, the heating and water pipes in buildings at Gagetown are so corroded that they need replacement, and the masonry on the Halifax armoury is in danger of falling on pedestrians. The army alone needs $1.6 billion to get its buildings into good repair, and hundreds of millions more to do environmental work on firing ranges and riverbeds in training areas.

The object in having the Canadian Forces is that they should protect Canada and make a difference when they serve abroad. It is highly unlikely that these forces will be large enough in the near future to have an impact in terms of numbers. It is, however, possible that they can make a difference qualitatively. That should be the aim. Strategist Colin Gray wrote a decade ago that "a Canada that cannot afford a large quantity has no prudent choice other than to pursue a force structure with a quality that yields high strategic leverage." He was right. If we play our hand well, we can advance our nation's interests with the military assets we can put on the table. We might also be able to defend ourselves better than we can today.

229

*   *   *

How do we budget for these needs? We need a plan and, ideally, a defence review will lay out how we get from the unhappy present to a better future. We need a Prime Minister and government that will commit themselves to moving Canada from its annual 1.1 percent of GDP today towards defence spending of 2 to 2.5 percent of GDP, roughly the average expenditure of NATO nations. This would mean that Canada must budget an additional many billions more each year for the foreseeable future. These sums must also be regularly adjusted upward for inflation and allow for pay raises for members of the Canadian Forces.*

I know the money needed is a staggering sum; I also know these figures are not wholly realistic in our present Canada. The money is not required all at once—it takes years to bring a major weapons system into line—and even the personnel increases I propose will take four or five years to achieve. What we truly need is a plan, a chart for the way ahead to which the Prime Minister and his government will be committed, with guarantees, as hard and fast as they can be in

---

*In October 2003, the Conference Board of Canada presented its "annual national progress report," *Performance and Potential* (Ottawa 2003). The board called for Canada to increase its defence spending—which is good. But it projected a twelve-year forecast that saw Canada raising defence spending to 1.25 percent of GDP—an amount that is hopelessly inadequate to meet the Canadian Forces' needs to participate meaningfully in homeland and continental defence and to serve in coalitions of the willing.

our parliamentary system, that their plan will be fulfilled. I also know that the Mulroney government made this kind of commitment after the 1987 White Paper, but it lied. A new government might try to hold itself to a higher standard. We, the voters, must hold the government to its pledges.

Let me be very clear once more and state what should be obvious: even this additional spending will not produce immediate results. Increasing personnel strength cannot be accomplished at once, and the flood of retirements in the next five years from the aging officer and non-commissioned member corps will also have to be replaced by new recruits. It will not be easy in a competitive labour market, and the Canadian Forces is already being forced to offer enlistment bonuses, for example, to college graduates in Internet technology ($10,000–20,000), engineering ($40,000), and medicine ($225,000). Large equipment purchases can take five to ten years—the Canadian Patrol Frigates were planned in the 1970s, built in the 1980s, and delivered in the 1990s—and politics will always interfere with sensible decisions, as Canada's experience with the replacement for Sea King helicopters should demonstrate.

But we must start somewhere, and we must start now. We need to decide today on the equipment we will need tomorrow, and we must begin a phased process of recruiting the kinds of servicemen and women we will need.

Again, let me state precisely what I mean. *Now* does not

231

mean five years after the new leader takes power; if so, there will be nothing left on which to build. *Now* means just as soon as the defence review is completed—which must be no later than the end of 2004. Indeed, the new Prime Minister needs to take some decisions, like the long overdue one to purchase new helicopters, even before the defence review is set in train. Chrétien set the tone for his dreadful decade in power by cancelling the EH-101 helicopter purchase. Martin should set the tenor of his government by buying the very best helicopter on the market for the air force in his first sixty days in office.

Our nation's leaders must understand that Canada is unlikely ever to be required to fight on its own. "The CF," said a National Defence paper on Strategic Capability Planning, "lacks the capability to achieve operational goals by itself in international situations. This is unlikely to change." That may be unfortunate, but it is surely a correct analysis. We will join coalitions, just as we did in both world wars and in Korea, the first Gulf War, and in Kosovo. Nothing forces us to be among the willing parties to a particular coalition, of course, but it will frequently be in our national interests to participate. Government must weigh such decisions closely and understand—and ensure the Canadian people understand—the consequences of its choices to participate or not. And government similarly must ensure that Canadians are able to operate jointly with our friends when the decision is to participate. If our leaders have confidence in their military, that attitude will help them decide whether to join coalitions. The responsibility for creating a usable force clearly rests with government in the first instance. The politicians control the purse and, if they underfund the Canadian Forces, they ought not to be surprised if the weapon they have at their disposal in a crisis is blunt.

The leadership of the Canadian Forces has its own responsibilities. One is that it must meet the requirement for a well-educated officer and non-commissioned member corps. The days are long gone when all a soldier needed was guts. Now education and the capacity to think are essential for all members of the Canadian Forces, and lifetime learning has to be a part of the military. With the Revolution in Military Affairs harnessing precision weapons and high-tech equipment with information technology and rapid communications, this requirement is more necessary than ever for all ranks. A military that lacks the trained personnel will not be able to act and react quickly enough to survive and prevail on the battlefield of tomorrow.

Such a force will not be easy to achieve in Canada—even if we can find the money for it—because anti-education biases continue to be strong in the military. In 1947 the Chief of the General Staff, Lieutenant-General Charles Foulkes, said that he wanted a bachelor's degree as the minimum for officers because of "the increasing requirements . . . for highly trained personnel due to the increasing complexity of modern warfare." A bachelor's degree was necessary if the army was "to be competitively efficient." Today, in a much more technologically driven world, 75.6 percent of Canadian Forces officers have undergraduate degrees, but only 11.7 percent have graduate degrees; seventy of seventy-three generals and admirals hold undergraduate degrees, and 39 percent of officers above the rank of colonel have graduate degrees.* There has been substantial progress in the last few years, and the Canadian Forces has created the Canadian Defence Academy to coordinate the educational efforts of its members. This is all to the good, and so is the government decision that officers who aspire to high rank will need a graduate degree to get there. Some of these degrees should be technical in nature, but there will always be a need for officers with a humanities and social sciences bent. The Canadian Forces, historically, has largely ignored this point.

---

*This record is a substantial change from 1997, when Defence Minister Doug Young asked four academics (Desmond Morton, David Bercuson, Albert Legault, and me) to offer advice on the future of the Canadian Forces. All four—quite independently—pointed to the lack of education in the officer corps as a cause of problems and something to be remedied. In my report, I said: "The CF has a remarkably ill-educated officer corps, surely one of the worst in the Western world." In 1997, 53.29 percent of officers had undergraduate degrees and only 6.79 percent graduate degrees, so the improvement has been real. The test for the forces will be to continue to improve and not to fall into the temptation to give officers credit for non-academic courses in field latrine-digging so they can punch their ticket with master's degrees.

The object of education in and for the forces is to produce junior and senior officers who know the military profession and have mastered its skills. But knowledge of tactics, technology, and the ability to process data is not enough. The officer must also understand the world, the nation, and the society in which she or he lives, as well as the societies in which the forces might serve. The officer must be connected to the history and heritage of Canada and the Canadian Forces. What we require, in effect, are military intellectuals, not just technicians of death. The American scholar Richard Gabriel noted: "A member of a profession is not merely a technician; a true member of the military profession must be a humanist." And a true professional must know how to question the received wisdom and how to tell the truth to his superiors. Education can help teach those skills.

The military, however, needs more than education. Like other professions, it must have an ethos. The motto of the Royal Military College of Canada is "Truth, Duty, Valour," which is not a bad place to begin. The motto of the United States Military Academy, West Point, is "Duty, Honour, Country," again not a bad starting point, not least because it states that "country," the nation, matters. In Canada, still torn between French- and English-Canadian attitudes to nationhood, we have tended not to wear our heart on our national sleeve. But the duty of every member of the Canadian Forces is to serve Canada, and members cannot be torn in their

235

allegiance. A proper motto for the Canadian Forces would stress Country, Valour, Truth, and Duty. The forces' 1997 Statement of Defence Ethics proclaims "Service, Honour, Commitment" as the watchwords of the military. Though there is nothing wrong with those words, nor with the statement's ritual bow to bilingualism, multiculturalism, Canadian values, family, and voluntarism, it reads as though it was written for an office full of parole board employees or social workers rather than a military.

Command is still about leadership, and leadership is about courage, sacrifice, integrity, personal responsibility, and will. Ethics, in other words, determines everything. It is difficult for officers to earn loyalty from those they command and, among other qualities, it demands high standards of behaviour. Arizona Senator John McCain, a US Navy pilot and long-time prisoner of war in Vietnam, has written about the officer's creed. An officer, he said, "must not lie, steal, or cheat—ever. He keeps his word, whatever the cost. He must not shirk his duties no matter how difficult or dangerous they are. His life is ransomed to his duty." Furthermore, "an officer accepts the consequences of his actions. . . . For the obedience he is owed by his subordinates, an officer accepts certain solemn obligations to them in return, and an officer's obligations to enlisted men are the most solemn of all." To McCain, "any officer who stains his honour by violating these standards forfeits the respect of his fellow officers and no longer deserves to be included in their ranks." These are all old-fashioned virtues that ring strangely in the cynical twenty-first century. Yet officers put the men and women they command in peril, and without a sense of honour and self-worth, they cannot do so in good conscience. In the 1990s some Canadian officers lost their honour. Those who lead the Canadian Forces in future can never allow that to recur.

If the Canadian Forces is to be the effective national military it used to be and must be tomorrow, its education and training, just as much as its equipment and conditions of service, need to be the very best. I do not want anyone but the best to lead my nation into war; I want none but the ablest to take my grandchildren into battle. This standard should matter to all Canadians, and it is not good enough for you and me to turn away or to say we will never be threatened. We are threatened and we will be, and pretending otherwise has led to the election of shameless, useless politicians who send our men and women to fly in forty-year-old helicopters and into battle driving twenty-year-old unarmoured Iltis vehicles. We need the best Canadian Forces we can have, and we need better politicians to get it for us. Nothing will happen unless we have a more aware electorate. You and I killed the Canadian military. Only you and I can restore it by telling our Prime Minister and our Members of Parliament that this restoration is essential.

The Prime Minister and his Ministers of Foreign Affairs and National Defence must lead. It is their responsibility to explain to Canadians, English- and French-speaking, why we need military forces and how they propose to use them. They must talk about Canada's national interests and how our sovereignty can only be protected and enhanced by cooperating where necessary with our neighbours and friends overseas. They must educate the voters, not pander to them. And they must do so to voters in Salmon Arm, Moosonee, Chicoutimi, and Moncton alike. We have not had a Prime Minister since Louis St. Laurent who went to the people to explain the realities of the world and to educate. Leaders are supposed to lead, and our last Prime Minister surely failed to do so. We need one who will.

We Canadians always assume that we live in God's country and that we will always be secure and safe, well protected in our prosperity. But the world is still a dangerous place—after September 11, who can doubt it? At some point, Canada's national interests will require us to be prepared to fight to protect our security, and it won't help us much then to prattle about our values and principles to those who would do us harm. We need a capable Canadian Forces to fight for us, and it is only sensible today to prepare for whatever the future may bring. If we pay now in dollars, we may not have to pay so heavily in the future with the lives of our young men and women. Canadians, it's up to us.

Afterword

IN MANY OF THE INTERVIEWS he gave after the report of his Afghanistan Panel appeared in late January 2008, John Manley made it crystal-clear that Canada's mission in Kandahar supports the United Nations Charter. As a card-carrying Liberal and former deputy prime minister, Manley did not hesitate to add that "Lester Pearson's fingerprints are all over the charter." He was right. Pearson's hand was evident in all the decisions and policies that established not only the UN Charter but all the fundamental Canadian foreign policy values that we cherish. They are liberal values and they have been Liberal values too.

I have half-called Pearson one of the "killers" of the Canadian military in this book, but I readily concede that in supporting peacekeeping he was not aiming directly at the nation's ability to fight, as some other prime ministers were. I remember that Mike Pearson served in the Great War in a hospital unit and as a trainee pilot in the Royal Flying Corps. He saw the death of his generation and the loss of many close friends. He joined the Department of External Affairs late in the 1920s, and he watched the failure of appeasement during the Great Depression. As a senior diplomat in London, Ottawa, and Washington during the years of the Second World War, he was one of the Canadians who helped to hold together the Allied coalition that defeated Hitler.

And I know that he drew the right lessons from the Second World War. Collective security was the answer to aggression, and the UN Charter called for the nations of the world to unite to crush those countries that disturbed the peace. But the incipient Cold War and the Great Power veto regularly wielded by the Soviet Union paralyzed the UN, and Pearson became one of those Canadians present at the creation of the North Atlantic Treaty. If the UN as a whole could not guarantee peace and security—and by 1948–49 it seemed clear that it could not—then the Western democracies would do it. By 1951, with Pearson now foreign minister in the Liberal government of Louis St. Laurent, Canada had dispatched 10,000 soldiers and airmen to Western Europe to face Moscow's armies, and it began devoting more than 7 percent of its Gross Domestic Product to defence. Today in 2008 we struggle to spend 1.3 percent of the GDP on the Canadian Forces.

When North Korea invaded South Korea in 1950, the

Soviet Union was fortuitously boycotting the Security Council, and for once the United Nations could act. Under Pearson's strong lead, Canada contributed a brigade group of infantry, ships, and air force transports. The United States ran the UN effort in Korea (and paid, along with the South Koreans, the heaviest price in lives), but collective security rescued a country from certain subjugation. Then, after Moscow developed a strategic air force that could attack North America with nuclear weapons, Pearson supported the construction of radar warning lines, the strengthening of defence relations with the United States, and the beginnings of negotiations for a joint air defence organization, the North American Air Defence Command (NORAD).

In other words, Pearson was no pacifist. He was a nationalist and an internationalist. He wanted Canada to have influence in Washington, with NATO, and at the UN; he wanted his country to play a strong role; and he understood that this favoured land had to work with its friends, especially the United States, to guarantee its security. He supported increasing defence budgets and raising troop numbers, and he understood that Canada sometimes had to be prepared to fight to defend its national interests. To Pearson, political, economic, and military strength, along with strategic alliances, were the keys to advancing Canadian national interests and securing Canada's place in the councils of the democracies.

241

Of course, in 1956, Pearson also played a central role in patching together a deal that "resolved" the crisis caused by the Anglo-French-Israeli invasion of Egypt. His idea of a United Nations Emergency Force made it possible for the invaders to withdraw and froze the situation on the ground. Pearson won the Nobel Peace Prize for his extraordinary efforts at the UN, and after that triumph Canadians began to believe fervently that peacekeeping was their invention and that Canadians did the UN's work better than any others.

This was a noble ideal, and conflict resolution became a Canadian value right up there—for a time—with collective security, defence preparation, and cooperation with Canada's allies. Peacekeeping appealed to Canadians because it was useful and because it seemed to differentiate us from the "warlike" Americans. After a time it began to appeal to our governments because it was far easier on hard-pressed budgets than purchasing heavy weaponry, and the 1990s development of a Canadian human security agenda by the Chrétien government fit seamlessly into this post-Pearsonian mental construct. Over the decades, the hard-edged values that Lester B. Pearson stood for so strongly began to fade in the Canadian memory and from the Liberal Party credo. All that remained was peacekeeping.

There is some irony in the fact that today the Stéphane Dion Liberals and the Jack Layton NDPers talk only of non-combat roles for Canadian troops in Afghanistan, often incorrectly invoking Pearson's memory and talking of peace-keeping as they do so. Mike Pearson was not a one-note, blue-beret advocate, however, demanding a UN force for every occasion. Curiously, it is Stephen Harper and the Conservative government who are taking the Pearsonian path in 2008: trying to give the Afghan people the human security and development they want and need while being prepared to fight alongside our friends against a fundamentalist, totalitarian Taliban.

John Manley's report got it right. Traditional peace-keeping cannot be practised in Kandahar now because there is no peace to keep there. But what we do "can affect Canada's reputation in the world . . . our influence in international affairs. . . ." Manley remembered the real Pearsonian legacy of careful judgment, resolve, and strength. Regrettably, many Canadians, looking at only part of it, have forgotten the rest.

JLG
Toronto, February 2008

Acknowledgements

I AM very fortunate to have Linda McKnight as my literary agent. She suggested this topic and title, and she and Phyllis Bruce of HarperCollins believed that the book, like *Who Killed Canadian History?* written a few years ago, might reach a large audience and have some useful impact on public debate. Phyllis Bruce and Rosemary Shipton, who worked on my prose, are the best of editors, and I am grateful, yet again, for their skill. Dean Oliver of the Canadian War Museum provided the Department of National Defence fiscal data and the Canadian Forces personnel numbers from one of the best research units anywhere. I am especially grateful to Patricia Grimshaw at the war museum. Alexis Apps at the Canadian Defence and Foreign Affairs Institute in Calgary assisted as well.

I owe thanks to David Bercuson, Robert Millar, Desmond

ACKNOWLEDGEMENTS

Morton, Dean Oliver, Roger Sarty, and Norman Hillmer, all of whom have assisted in many ways in discussions over the years. Dean, Norman, and David read the entire text and fired repeated and well-aimed salvoes at me. I ducked when I could and retreated when they forced me out of my positions. They are good friends, stern critics, and far wiser than I am. My thanks to them all.

JLG
Toronto, November 2003

Index